ON THE JOB
Survival or Satisfaction

BY JERRY AND MARY WHITE

NAVPRESS ®
A MINISTRY OF THE NAVIGATORS
P.O. BOX 6000, COLORADO SPRINGS, COLORADO 80934

The Navigators is an international Christian organization. Jesus Christ gave His followers the Great Commission to go and make disciples (Matthew 28:19). The aim of The Navigators is to help fulfill that commission by multiplying laborers for Christ in every nation.

NavPress is the publishing ministry of The Navigators. NavPress publications are tools to help Christians grow. Although publications alone cannot make disciples or change lives, they can help believers learn biblical discipleship, and apply what they learn to their lives and ministries.

CONTENTS

AUTHORS

Jerry White is General Director of The Navigators. He holds a Ph.D. in astronautics. During thirteen years with the United States Air Force, he served as a space mission controller at Cape Canaveral. He also served as associate professor of astronautics at the United States Air Force Academy for six years, and co-authored a nationally recognized textbook on astrodynamics. He resigned from active duty in 1973.

Mary Ann Knutson White attended Northwestern Bible College and the University of Washington. She holds a degree in English from the University of Colorado, and has worked as a secretary in government and private industry.

The Whites' first contact with The Navigators was at the University of Washington. They later helped begin Navigator ministries at the Air Force Academy in 1964 and at Purdue University in 1966.

Jerry and Mary are the authors of *Friends and Friendship*. Jerry has also written *Choosing Plan A in a Plan B World*; *Honesty, Morality, and Conscience*; *The Church and the Parachurch: An Uneasy Marriage*; and *The Power of Commitment*.

INTRODUCTION

It was 10:30 p.m. when the phone on my desk rang. My first reaction was irritation. It had been a long day of mind-stretching work and complex personal interaction. I was tired, and I was in the middle of a serious counseling session. Reluctantly I picked up the phone.

"Hello, Jerry. This is Brian Wilson."

A pang of embarrassment passed through me. I had neglected to return his call of just an hour ago. I sensed an emptiness in his voice that told me something was wrong. I made a lame apology for not returning his call.

"I'm being fired from my job," he said in an emotionally flat tone.

Knowing him, I was amazed. "Why?"

He had been confronted by his boss and was told his work did not meet even minimum standards. Expecting he would make excuses and tell me the reasons the boss was wrong, I asked, "Do you agree with him?"

"Yes, I do. I think I may be incompetent. Maybe I should quit now. Maybe I'm in the wrong line of work. In your seminar on work you mentioned this kind of situation.

7

Can we get together to talk?"

Was God playing a bitter joke on him? He was twelve years into his career, held a master's degree, and had a good record up to this point. Now it was all ruined—or was it?

Brian is different from many who speak to me about work only in that his frustrations and problems have reached crisis level. What about the insecurity feelings of the salesman in that same seminar who was trying to figure out how to survive, using Christian principles, in his dog-eat-dog business? Or the mechanic who countered the salesman's comments with his dilemma of "the common workers" trying to keep their jobs while competing with people who cheat on production and performance to make themselves look good?

A few years ago I was speaking to a group of single adults about living the Christian life in the real world. I casually included a brief session on their relationships to their jobs. A time bomb exploded! There were many questions, strong feelings of frustration, and a general sense of dissatisfaction with their success in integrating their jobs with their Christian lives. It was obvious that I had touched a sensitive nerve. The interest was so intense that I continued the discussion the next week. I tried to find resource material for them, but very little was available—especially for the Christian man or woman.

I began to speak on the specific topic of work to other groups—students, couples, older workers, homemakers, laborers, and professionally trained people. Their reaction was virtually the same—intense interest, underlying dissatisfaction, frustration, and uncertainty about the importance of work to the Christian. Yet many greatly enjoyed their work and had successfully integrated it into their lives. Their probing questions, the wise insights, and my personal experience and study of the Scriptures gave birth to this material.

When *Your Job—Survival or Satisfaction?* was published, we began to speak and teach broadly on the subject. In those sessions, we discovered many questions and problems not fully addressed in the book. The questions on ethics gave rise to *Honesty, Morality, and Conscience.* Other problems also clouded the specific issue of work, namely mid-life and mid-career frustrations. Some of these issues were addressed in *The Christian in Mid-Life.*

This book contains what we view by experience as the best and most pertinent material from *Your Job—Survival or Satisfaction?* and *The Christian in Mid-Life* (both are now out of print). A moderate amount of material has been added and some has been deleted in order to focus on the most crucial issues and solutions for the Christian in today's marketplace.

We have personally struggled with the pressures of secular work, family needs, and personal ministry. The concepts taught here are not just theory, but a result of personal experience and the counsel and input of others who have faced work circumstances that we have not. The Navigators, with their historical focus on the layperson and emphasis on servanthood and excellence in work, have profoundly influenced our thinking.

Chapter One

THE FRUSTRATIONS AND CHALLENGES OF WORK

Work fills almost half of every person's waking lifetime. Working is the one constant of all mankind's activities.

Man's response to work spans a kaleidoscope of feelings and attitudes. One person may love work—savoring it daily, motivated to do more, mesmerized by its possibilities, and even consumed by its challenges. This person almost lives to work.

But for every person who loves work, there are many others who simply tolerate it as a necessity of life, finding it onerous, boring, and unfulfilling. They get up and head to work with reluctance, often subjecting themselves to unjust bosses, uninteresting tasks, or dehumanizing work conditions. They work only to make a living.

In the world of work we encounter failure and success, fear and anticipation, boredom and challenge, conflict and harmony, injustice and justice. Often the same person will find all of these elements in the same job over a period of years. Life, especially life at work, is filled with the unknown.

The motivated and successful often pursue their work

with the wrong motives and end up in spiritual and personal calamity. The unmotivated and unsuccessful often respond with bitterness and apathy, which corrode their spiritual and personal happiness.

We see people limited by their education, skills, background, or opportunity. We see others with all of these advantages who are still unmotivated and unhappy. We also see people of great limitations who find happiness and fulfillment by making life a daily adventure. Advantages and abilities certainly do not necessarily lead to success and happiness.

Life at work is filled with dilemmas and contradictions. Work and the world bring us face to face with ourselves, revealing facets of our being that we do not like to see. We see greed and ambition, pride and anger, frustration and doubt, all rearing their ugly heads, while at the same time we want to see the proper fruit of the Spirit growing in our lives. So guilt and conscience begin to drain us emotionally in our desperate attempt to solve the incessant combat between the secular and the spiritual aspects of living.

As we discuss this dilemma with people, we find that few are completely satisfied with their jobs and few know where work should fit with the rest of their lives. Personal conflicts, overwork, overambition, financial pressure, fear of unemployment, boredom, lack of opportunity, and countless other problems plague their existence. Some like work too much and neglect the family; others hate work and dread every day; some ignore the problems and go through the day like robots.

Engineers, machinists, homemakers, secretaries, draftsmen, lawyers, salesmen, assembly-line workers, and managers—regardless of the job, the frustrations remain the same. Many spend their lives trying to escape from the stark reality of pouring forty percent of their working lifetime into a job they hate. We give the majority of our adult lives to our work, but too often conflict comes with the job. The work is either too difficult or too boring. It is too demanding or offers no challenge. The pay may be poor or if the salary is adequate, the work takes too much time. The unacceptable alternative is unemployment.

It is even worse if you are a Christian and are *supposed* to enjoy life and not have the problems and concerns common to the world. That is good in theory, but in reality it is obvious that Christians also have fears, unpaid bills, overextended charge accounts, conflicts on the job, consuming ambition to get ahead, a thirst for greater financial freedom, or just a desire for a "little" taste of the luxuries of life.

In the midst of these circumstances we want to find biblical *and* practical solutions to the problem of how a job fits in with family and ministry. The issue cannot be avoided by going into "full-time" Christian work; then *ministry is the job*, and suddenly a new set of even more complex problems arises. For instance, what if you do not like some of the requirements of your ministry-job? If you cannot successfully blend your Christian life and your secular job, almost certainly you will not succeed in vocational Christian service.

After thirteen and a half years in my secular job, I did change to vocational Christian service. The pressures remained as heavy. I still struggled to sustain a consistent devotional life. The conflicts and problems were still present. People had expressed gratitude for all I did in my ministry as a layman; now I am expected to do it—and to do it better than before. After all, I have more time, so I should do more.

I am still the same person with the same motives, attitudes, and limitations. Yet the lessons I learned in coping with my secular job are the same ones that help me now. This book is a reflection of many of those experiences that we faced individually and as a couple.

Many questions and issues confront Christians in secular jobs:

▶ What can I do when I do not like my work but cannot change because of educational or financial restrictions?

▶ How can I do well in my job without "selling my soul" to the company?

▶ Why do I have so many conflicts with my supervisors?

▶ I feel guilty working at a secular job when I know I could be on the missionfield. I'm convicted whenever I attend a missions conference. What should I do?

▶ My job is so demanding that it requires fifteen or twenty extra hours a week just to keep up. It is hurting my family, but how can I refuse to do what my boss asks of me?

▶ I am always running scared, because if I do not do my job well, there are ten people waiting to take it. How can I overcome this anxiety and trust God?

▶ We have three children in college, so both my husband and I are working. But it really bothers me, since I have been admonished that this is wrong. Is it?

▶ I have tried many times to give the proper priorities to my family and to some type of outreach ministry, but I fail every time. My priorities get fouled up, my schedule gets disrupted. How can I attain consistency?

▶ By the time I work forty or more hours in my job, go to three or four church meetings a week, and carry out my church responsibilities, I have no time left for my family. What should I do?

▶ The children are in their teens and are rebelling. My

job is finally paying off, and to succeed I need to give it one hundred percent. Should I give up my career just for the children?

▶ How do I decide to change jobs or location?

▶ Is it wrong to be ambitious?

▶ Is there anything wrong with being "just a housewife"?

▶ I have been to several family seminars and am deeply convicted about my relationship to my family. But still, I have to put bread on the table. How can I achieve a balance?

▶ Is there anything wrong with working hard to get nice things for the family?

▶ If I did everything I am told I "must" do to be a successful parent, employee, and Christian, I would need one hundred extra hours in each week! Can it really be done?

▶ I am "just" a factory worker. What good am I to the Kingdom of God?

This book deals with these questions. It will not give black-and-white, dogmatic answers to each one, but will provide scriptural and practical principles from which you can personally seek God's will.

For clarity, we need to define the key words in this book:

Job or work: That task or skill that is the main source of your financial income—what you are expected to do to receive pay.

Family: Your wife or husband, children, and the activities arising from your responsibilities to them.

Ministry: Your spiritual outreach to those outside your family. It may be through your church, in your neighborhood, or through other Christian organizations, or endeavors you have personally arranged.

Some may say "my job is my ministry!" or "my family is my ministry!" That is true. But for the purposes of this discussion, we will simply use the term *ministry* to refer to outside endeavors.

THE CHRISTIAN VIEW OF SOCIETY

Before looking at the Christian view of work, we need to ask whether there is a Christian view of society. Is all society bad? Should prophecies of doom govern our thinking about the world? No society in history has been truly Christian. Not even Israel maintained a godly perspective over an extended period of time. But all of us live in society with its problems, evils, and benefits.

Society becomes "Christian" only as individuals in it become Christians and multiply. Then they may be able to permeate it with Christian views of government, business, economics, politics, and ethics. But that will never happen if Christians hibernate from society. We need to be in the world, but not conformed to the world (Romans 12:2).

Let's look at several things the Bible teaches about human society.

Society is established by God. God established human society with certain objectives. In Genesis 1:26 man was to "rule . . . over all the earth." He was to "be fruitful and multiply, and fill the earth, and subdue it" (verse 28). God also established concepts of government, order, and justice. These were distinct from spiritual rules of worship. So God's objectives for human society were:

▶ to glorify Himself in all creation (Psalm 19:1-6);
▶ to establish authority and order (Deuteronomy 16:18-20);

▶ to meet man's physical needs (Genesis 1:29-30, Deuteronomy 15:2-14);
▶ to establish concepts of justice and man's relationships (Exodus 20:1-17);
▶ to bless all mankind through the promises to Abraham fulfilled in Christ (Genesis 12:3).

Thus God established society as His means for the prosecution of all human relationships.

Society is not inherently evil. Human society is not inherently wrong or evil. People do evil things, not society; but people constitute the society. By God's sovereignty we were each born into a segment of total society and cannot escape from it, nor should we want to. However, we as Christians want to influence our society for good and not allow society to influence us adversely.

It is true that the world system (cosmos) is condemned in the New Testament. But the world system is not the same as society. Society is a grouping of people around a common goal (e.g., survival, business, or protection). This society can be deeply influenced by Satan's way of thinking as expressed in the world system. The results of evil influences permeate some societies more than others, and it is more difficult for the Christian to be a full participant in them.

Society provides an environment. Human society provides an environment in which God confronts man. Human society is the mechanism by which man lives and functions as a human being. In this process God then confronts each person about his purpose in life and his personal relationship to God and Christ. The prime tools of this confrontation are:

▶ the creation (general revelation); God's power and majesty, shown in creation, draw men and women to seek Him (Romans 1:19-20).

▶ the Scriptures (specific revelation); the Bible forms the primary "hard" evidence we have regarding God's master plan for all mankind—individual as well as the entire society. We must always keep Scripture as an integral part of our confrontation with society.

▶ individual Christians sharing their faith (personalized revelation); people may reject creation and the Bible, but they cannot reject the living evidence of one person's life and experience.

Society perpetuates the race. Human society is self-perpetuating and self-preserving. Everyone takes part in the sustenance of everyone else. Imagine several families performing certain functions for each other, such as growing food, sewing clothes, and repairing homes. Food is needed, so some are farmers. People get sick, so some are doctors. Houses are needed, so some are carpenters. In a primitive sense, specialized labor is needed for items that meet physical needs. Industrialization, corporations, and competition have changed the face of this simple trading, but the idea remains the same.

Every person makes a contribution to society. Every occupation fills a need, or at least a want. Ultimately we are all dependent on one another.

So what is the Christian view of society? Society was divinely ordained by God for the purpose of sustaining His human creation. Therefore we must be vital and active participants in every area of society to reach people for Christ and to influence it to be more "Christian" in character. We are an *anti-pollution* influence on our society.

You may say, "That's a little too academic. I'm stuck here, so just tell me how to survive." Yes, but you must realize where you are "stuck" is part of God's plan for you.

Society provides the context for witness. You are a key

part of God's plan for reaching a pagan society. His plan is for you to be *salt* and *light* in the society.

> You are the salt of the earth; but if the salt has become tasteless, how will it be made salty again? It is good for nothing anymore, except to be thrown out and trampled under foot by men. You are the light of the world. A city set on a hill cannot be hidden. Nor do men light a lamp, and put it under the peck-measure, but on the lampstand; and it gives light to all who are in the house. Let your light shine before men in such a way that they may see your good works, and glorify your Father who is in heaven. (Matthew 5:13-16)

Have you ever salted your food and accidentally dumped too much in one place? You could hardly stand to taste it, could you? Salt must gently permeate the whole. Concentrated, it tastes terrible; scattered out, it gives flavor and savor to the food. So God wants Christians spread out in every neighborhood, institution, and occupation. Non-Christians should *taste* Christ by observing your life. What kind of flavor do you give as you work in your job?

Salt has another use. Gathered in large quantities, it is a preservative. Unfortunately we often interpret salting society as Christians gathering together. The result? Preserved or pickled Christians! We must be out in the middle of society, where we find the real needs. In many ways Christians in the society have a preserving influence, much as the presence of a few righteous people would have preserved Sodom (Genesis 18:16-33).

But salt also makes one *thirsty.* Tavern owners use that fact regularly by putting out salty peanuts or pretzels for people to eat freely (the customers become thirsty and purchase more beverages). Our lives should make people hunger and thirst for our Lord Jesus Christ.

What about *light?* You are to be that too—in the middle of darkness. People need to *see* Christ in us by how we work, act, and react. When a candle is covered with a cup, it goes out. When you cover up as a Christian, you risk spiritual stagnation. Be out in the open, vulnerable to the scrutiny of every nonChristian. One of the primary purposes of doing well in your job is to draw people's attention to God, not yourself.

Allow people to *taste* and *see* Christ in you. Be salt: permeate society with the taste of Christ, causing people to thirst for Him. Be light: let society see Christ in you as you live and work.

Can a Christian actually change even part of society? Here is a striking example.

Luming was a petite Filipino in her early thirties, very feminine, with a quiet, modest demeanor. A competent architect working for the government, until recently she was in the department that designed all the schools and government buildings in the province of Rizal. After design, it was the procedure that the projects be turned over to another department for bidding and construction.

Out of personal interest she followed the progress of one set of buildings designed to be built on a landfill area. She noticed that the contract was made for a much lower price than it would cost to build. Upon writing a memo to her boss, she was told, "Just mind your own business." But being a committed Christian and a citizen, it was her business.

Luming visited the site and found that the contractor had moved the building to a place not requiring a landfill—but it was not government property. This allowed the contractor to bid lower and still pocket a good deal of money. She marched up to the contractor and told him to cease and desist on the building. He told her it was out of her hands and none of her business. Obviously government officials were involved in a payoff.

Next Luming addressed a letter to the governor. It was bounced back before reaching him, with the warning that if she persisted in sending the memo through, her brother would lose his job. After discussing the situation with her brother, who was also a Christian, she sent the memo through. She was called in to explain the matter to the governor, and the contract was rescinded. Her brother did lose his job, and she was warned by others that if she persisted in this kind of honesty, she would never be promoted.

But Luming chose to live her life before God in the knowledge that she will ultimately answer to Him. Her department allowed no dishonest transactions, through the influence of one woman who based her work on God's principles.

Ironically, Luming was promoted and became division chief in charge of low-cost housing and subdivisions in the entire province. She also held a second responsibility as assistant to the governor's chief executive office. Luming has changed her society by demonstrating a unique blend of professional competence and godly commitment.

Chapter Two

THE SCRIPTURAL BASIS FOR WORK

M any Christians harbor the sneaking suspicion that work is more God's curse than God's blessing. This view is reinforced by the insidious separation of the secular and the sacred. Many Christians are criticized for their religious fervor on Sunday and their seeming abandonment of Christian principles in the work place—giving rise to the many accusations of hypocritical behavior.

Is "secular" work really part of God's plan? Does it take second place to our spiritual activities? Is one more spiritual while worshiping than when working? We need to know God's mind on these issues. If, after all, work is second best in God's plans, we ought to avoid it at all costs!

To answer this we can only appeal to the Scriptures to discover God's view of work in a fallen world.

THE VIEW OF WORK IN THE OLD TESTAMENT

In the Old Testament work was highly honored, especially skilled labor. People who had the ability to make things— such as silversmiths, stonecutters, carpenters, cloth makers—were especially respected.

Throughout the Old Testament the following principles stand out:

Work Is an Integral Part of Life

This concept stemmed from the high view of responsibility to one's own family. Failing to provide for them made a man an outcast from the community. Every Jewish child was required to train for a manual occupation. William Barclay noted:

> To a Jew work was essential—work was of the essence of life. The Jews had a saying that "he who does not teach his son a trade teaches him to steal." A Jewish rabbi was the equivalent to a college lecturer or professor, but according to Jewish law he must take not a penny for teaching; he must have a trade at which he worked with his hands and by which he supported himself. So there were rabbis who were tailors and shoemakers and barbers and bakers and even performers. Work to a Jew was life.[1]

The fall of man altered the difficulty of work, but not its value. Many Christians are under the impression that the fall of man in the Garden of Eden put a curse on work. Let's examine that passage more carefully.

> Then the LORD God said to the woman, "What is this you have done?" And the woman said, "The serpent deceived me, and I ate." . . . To the woman He said, "I will greatly multiply your pain in childbirth, in pain you shall bring forth children; yet your desire shall be for your husband, and he shall rule over you." Then to Adam He said, ". . . Cursed is the ground because of

you; in toil you shall eat of it all the days of your life. Both thorns and thistles it shall grow for you; and you shall eat the plants of the field; by the sweat of your face you shall eat bread, till you return to the ground, because from it you were taken; for you were dust, and to dust you shall return." (Genesis 3:13,16-19)

This passage does not teach that work as such is under a curse or the result of a curse any more than it teaches that child-bearing is cursed or that women are cursed. It teaches that from this time onward survival will be difficult without the lushness of the Garden of Eden and that death would be the ultimate end for all people. Until this time sickness, pain, and death were unknown.

But even more importantly, God ordained work as good before the Fall. In Genesis 2:15, we read, "Then the LORD God took the man and put him into the garden of Eden to cultivate it and to keep it."

The very first thing God gave man was a task or work! He had a job—to cultivate and keep the garden. Before God gave him Eve, He gave him work. It was part of God's plan from the beginning.

Everyone Should Work
There was honor in labor. Exodus 34:21 gives this com-mand: "You shall work six days, but on the seventh day you shall rest; even during plowing time and harvest you shall rest." Emphasis is usually placed on resting one day a week. But note that it says, "You *shall* work six days." That is a command, not a choice. Idleness was condemned. Every man contributed his part in supporting his family. In Prov-erbs 3:6-8 God commands us to observe the ant and learn: the ant works hard to gather food to sustain life. Remember that work in this age includes all that is involved in sustaining

a family, not just a job in a business. So today our six days include mowing the lawn, painting the house, and repairing the car. Work is clearly an essential part of life.

Working Hard Is Satisfying

The Proverbs are filled with admonitions about hard work. "He also who is slack in his work is brother to him who destroys" (18:9). "Laziness casts into a deep sleep, and an idle man will suffer hunger" (19:15). The Old Testament condemns laziness and commends hard work.

Man is not to dread labor, but to be fulfilled by the creation of his hands or mind. "The sleep of the working man is pleasant, whether he eats little or much" (Ecclesiastes 5:12). "In all labor there is profit" (Proverbs 14:23). "And I have seen that nothing is better than that man should be happy in his [work], for that is his lot" (Ecclesiastes 3:22).

All Legitimate Professions Were Honorable

We see approval of all kinds of work:

▶ laboring (1 Kings 5:7-18);
▶ manual skills (Exodus 36:1-2);
▶ business/managerial (Daniel, Moses);
▶ mental/scientific (Daniel).

Some professions were "illegal" or dishonorable. These included prostitution, lending at high interest, any business that cheated or took advantage of the poor, or any business conducted dishonestly.

THE VIEW OF WORK IN THE NEW TESTAMENT

Work is assumed in the New Testament to be a normal mode of life for everyone. None of the Old Testament concepts are repealed, but all are emphasized, with additional stress on the person's attitude toward his job and employer. So even in the context of grace, there is no escaping the responsibility of work. In fact, now it is not just work, but how *well* one does his job.

Consider these key principles in the New Testament:

No Work, No Eat

Second Thessalonians 3:10 says, "If anyone will not work, neither let him eat." That is a tough statement. Where is our social compassion? In a day of unemployment compensations and socialized subsidies, Paul would not be very popular at the polls with that platform—even among Christians. But it says, "If anyone *will* not work." This signifies that there is an option. Paul is not dealing with the sick, elderly, or disabled, who have no choice. This rule applies to an individual who decides not to work—who is too lazy, too choosy, or too undependable to hold a job. Verse 14 goes on to say that we are not to associate with the man who refuses to work and becomes a sponge to society. There are valid reasons for being unemployed, and we are responsible to uphold each other in those circumstances.

Provide for Your Family

"But if any one does not provide for his own, and especially for those of his household, he has denied the faith, and is worse than an unbeliever" (1 Timothy 5:8). That is a big responsibility. A Christian must provide for the physical needs of his family. If he does not, his testimony is ruined. The emphasis here is on needs, not luxuries. In any society the primary way to provide justly for the family is to work.

God certainly is sovereign, able to provide in any way He wishes—manna, gifts, government, or whatever—but in general, provision will result from work.

Be an Obedient and Submissive Employee

In Colossians 3:22, the Apostle Paul commands slaves to be obedient to their masters. In today's society this is speaking to the employee (though some employees probably feel more like slaves in their jobs). Can you be submissive and obedient while participating in strikes and protests and demanding your "rights"? There is no simple answer to that question. The key is to do what is legal in your society and does not conflict with Scripture, and to come to a personal conviction about your participation in these activities. But be sure you have a clear conscience before God in your actions (Acts 24:16).

What are your rights? Did Jesus demand His rights? The one clear guideline in your job is to be faithful, obedient, and submissive. To the soldier, John the Baptist commanded, "Be content with your wages" (Luke 3:14). When you obey the command to be submissive, you will be mistreated at times. In similar circumstances Jesus set this example: "While being reviled, He did not revile in return; while suffering, He uttered no threats, but kept entrusting Himself to Him who judges righteously" (1 Peter 2:23). On the other hand, in reaction to cheating and unlawful use of the Temple, He overturned the moneychangers' tables and drove them out (Matthew 12:12-13). Each circumstance must be decided on its own merits.

Be a Just and Fair Employer

"Masters, grant to your slaves justice and fairness, knowing that you too have a Master in heaven" (Colossians 4:1). If you are an employer, you have an even greater responsibility to be just and fair to those who work for you. You are to pay them their wages fairly and promptly (Leviticus 19:13). You are to look out for their concerns. You are to consider their rights and be responsive to their needs and requests.

Make Excellence Your Work Standard

Jesus worked as a carpenter—but He was not just a carpenter, He was God. Paul worked as a tentmaker—but he was not just a tentmaker, he was the apostle to the Gentiles. Peter worked as a fisherman—but he was not just a fisherman, he was the apostle to the Jews. Lydia worked as a cloth dyer—but she was not just a cloth dyer, she was a witness and a woman of hospitality. Do you think those persons followed these scriptural principles? Do you follow them?

A summary passage on work is 1 Thessalonians 4:11-12: "Make it your ambition to lead a quiet life and attend to your own business and work with your hands, just as we commanded you; so that you may behave properly toward outsiders and not be in any need."

We conclude that the reasons for work are to

▶ glorify God,
▶ provide for our family's needs,
▶ present a good reputation to the world.

Notice that personal fulfillment is not included.

EXCELLENCE IN WORK

▶ "I'd rather deal with nonChristians in business. Too many Christians have really disappointed me in their dealings."
▶ "He may be a Christian, but he really doesn't do good work."
▶ "He claims to be a Christian, but I know atheists who work harder and do better work than he does."

Have you heard statements like these? Of course you have. Sadly enough, they are often true. You may argue that there are many nonChristians who do poor work. True. But we are a "chosen" people; there is a special mark and responsibility on us as Christians. You cannot be just an ordinary worker. "Whatever you do, do your work heartily, as for the Lord rather than for men" (Colossians 3:23).

You represent Jesus Christ to the world, not just by your speech and morality, but also by your *work*. If you are *salt* and *light* to the world, you must be *salt* and *light* in your work, too.

Between my junior and senior years in college I worked for Boeing Aircraft Company as an engineering draftsman. As a Christian I felt the responsibility to witness to my coworkers, and witness I did—on the job, during work hours, when I and they were to be producing work for the company. What an impact I had! It was even noticed by the boss, who reprimanded me for not working! I learned a valuable lesson, but not till I had tarnished my "real" witness on the job. Moreover, no one came to Christ. In fact, I would hate to hear what they said behind my back.

> Do you see a man skilled in his work? He will stand before kings; he will not stand before obscure men. (Proverbs 22:29)

> I passed by the field of the sluggard, and by the vineyard of the man lacking sense; and behold, it was completely overgrown with thistles, its surface was covered with nettles, and its stone wall was broken down.
> When I saw, I reflected upon it; I looked, and received instruction. (Proverbs 24:30-32)

God expects excellence. He does not expect you to be a "superworker" or one who has no limitations; but He does expect you to do the best you possibly can.

What will be the results of your doing your work excellently? Here are a few of the possibilities:

▶ You will have a better witness.
▶ You will have more job security.
▶ You will be promoted or paid more.
▶ You will have greater job satisfaction.

As you see, there is much in it for you.

The Bible clearly teaches that work is right and good in life and in society and that it must be done God's way. But that knowledge alone cannot show you how to solve some of the knotty problems you are likely to encounter, so read on.

NOTES: 1. William Barclay, *Ethics in a Permissive Society* (New York: Harper & Row, 1971), page 94.

Chapter Three

THE CHRISTIAN VIEW OF CIRCUMSTANCES

From time to time, everyone encounters difficult—indeed, miserable—circumstances. Some people struggle with adverse conditions far more frequently than others. The job is too demanding, the relationships on the job are difficult, trouble is brewing in the home, work hours are too long, money is tight, you have lost your job, you dislike the community in which you live, or your work has become boring and dissatisfying. When one or more of these things happen, we are plagued with the malady that I call the "grass-is-greener syndrome."

THE GRASS-IS-GREENER SYNDROME

Do you believe that changing your circumstances will solve your problems? This course has been attempted many times and has failed, but still it is pursued even among those who have tried it. We mistakenly feel that the problem is outside ourselves and that changing our location, job, or surroundings will make things different. We make the change, but the problems return and we are no better off than before.

We are all familiar with the proverb that "the grass is greener on the other side of the fence." We feel if we could just be somewhere else, things would be better. But they seldom are. Changing your circumstances will not generally solve your problems. Most problems are of our own making or are generated within ourselves.

Could it be that God has placed you in some circumstances for your benefit and teaching? Could it be that He does not want you to escape, but to learn how to live in those circumstances? The immediate impulse in any difficulty is to run to avoid the situation. If we cannot run, we become bitter and complain about our plight. The bitterness deepens and we find ourselves in despair. In the whole process we lose our perspective of what God is doing in our lives. We question why God could let us experience these difficulties.

King Solomon spent his entire lifetime trying to find satisfying circumstances. He desperately searched for some situation or set of experiences that would make him happy. He never found them. His conclusion recorded in the book of Ecclesiastes was that "all is vanity." He tried to make circumstances fit his desires rather than allow God to be his total satisfaction in the existing situation.

Paul had the right response to his circumstances. He said, "I have learned to be content in whatever circumstances I am. I know how to get along with humble means, and I also know how to live in prosperity; in any and every circumstance I have learned the secret of being filled and going hungry, both of having abundance and suffering need" (Philippians 4:11-12). Paul had reconciled himself to reality.

REALITY—LIVING LIFE AS IT IS

Escaping from circumstances usually means escaping from reality. We do not want to face life as it really is. We live in the future hoping that things will change, or in the past wishing that things were as they used to be. To live full and meaningful lives, we must live in the present in light of the future.

If you are married and experiencing difficulties, you cannot go back to being single without great trauma and even more difficult circumstances. If you have children and that responsibility weighs heavily on you, you still must meet the needs of your family. If you are having problems now in your job situation, you will often encounter similar problems in another job. If you are having conflicts with people in your church, you will probably have conflicts in another church. Everywhere you turn, the pressure of reality continues to confront you.

But that is God's plan. God's objective is to use the pressures of real life to cause us to turn to Him. In John 16:33 Jesus promises constant pressure. "In the world you have tribulation, but take courage; I have overcome the world." The word *tribulation* is the same word used for pressing out the wine from the grapes. This verse could be translated, "In the world you have pressure." We will never be able to escape those pressures, but we can have peace and fulfillment in the midst of them. Jesus says to "take courage," not to "run away"; because He has overcome the world, we can successfully endure that stress.

The beginning of John 16:33 teaches that we can have peace in spite of pressure. The peace comes in knowing that God is in charge and all our circumstances are divinely ordained by Him. Your reaction to circumstances reveals your spiritual maturity. Do you get angry? Do you become discouraged? Are you fearful? Although it is wrong to be angry with God for a set of circumstances, it is not wrong to ask why they exist. God has some purpose in every event He brings into your life.

CIRCUMSTANCES—
GOD'S TRAINING PROGRAM FOR YOU

If anyone had a right to be bitter against God, it was Joseph (Genesis 37-47). He simply told the truth, and his brothers became furious and planned to kill him. Deciding that it would be wrong to take his life, they sold him as a slave into Egypt and deceived their elderly father into thinking he was dead. Joseph worked his way up in the household of Potiphar to a position of high responsibility. Moreover, he did this by excellent performance in his work and a right relationship with God. "And the LORD was with Joseph, so he became a successful man. And he was in the house of his master the Egyptian. Now his master saw that the LORD was with him and how the LORD caused all that he did to prosper in his hand" (Genesis 39:2-3).

Then Potiphar's wife tried to seduce Joseph. When he refused, she made a false accusation, and Potiphar dismissed Joseph from his job and threw him into prison. There, even as a prisoner, he rose to a position of responsibility. God brought the Pharaoh's baker and butler into prison, and Joseph interpreted each of their dreams. Later the Pharaoh himself called for Joseph to interpret his dream and subsequently made Joseph the second ruler in the entire land of Egypt.

What if Joseph had become bitter and had sulked and complained against God? Would he ever have won the respect of those around him? Probably not. In all these circumstances, he was treated unjustly, but God ultimately blessed him. Instead of getting an ulcer, he got honor. Instead of complaining, he complied. Instead of appealing through the courts, he became a faithful slave and servant. But Joseph could not have done this had he not understood that God had ordained the circumstances and was preparing him for the future. Are you willing to allow your circumstances to prepare you for the future?

Rather than giving you success and ease in all you do, God is first interested in changing your character to become more like Jesus Christ. Then He will use you to reach out to others.

▶ If you are having conflicts with your boss, God may be trying to teach you something about *biblical submission to authority.*

▶ If you are in very tight financial circumstances, God may be trying to teach you something about *generosity* or *materialism.*

▶ If you are in conflict with your husband or wife, God may be teaching you something about the *biblical view of marriage.*

▶ If you are being unjustly treated at your job, He may be teaching you how to *be at peace* in difficult circumstances.

▶ If you are bored and discouraged in your job, He may be teaching you something about *patience* and *perseverance.*

▶ If you are without a job, He may be teaching you *dependence on Him* and causing you to reevaluate your *priorities and objectives.*

▶ If you are under pressure on your job because you have not done your work well, He may be teaching you something about *faithfulness* and *dependability.*

▶ If you are experiencing fear and insecurity in your job, God may be teaching you *dependence on Him* and to find your *security in Him.*

This list could go on, but in all these circumstances the following key points begin to stand out:

▶ God is sovereign in your circumstances.

▶ Be patient in waiting for God to resolve the circumstance. Let Him get your attention so you can learn the lesson He intends to teach you.

▶ God wants to change your character and your attitude toward Him and toward others.

▶ God wants you to find your total peace and contentment in your relationship with Him, and through His Word and prayer.

Many know the words of Romans 8:28: "And we know that God causes all things to work together for good to those who love God, to those who are called according to His purpose." But do you know the experience of that verse? God has a specific purpose in every circumstance. The prerequisites are that you love God and are in His will right now. Romans 8:28 is not just a cop-out on reality or a glib reply to be given to others in distress. This verse causes us to understand that God is trying to get our attention and that He will ultimately turn adverse circumstances to good. He does not guarantee a total understanding of what He is doing and why, but He guarantees that He is acting on our behalf.

Are you in a particularly difficult circumstance? What can you do to discover what God is teaching you? Take a piece of paper and briefly answer these questions as a start:

1. What is the circumstance? Be brief, but specific.
2. How did the circumstance develop?
3. From your experience in the circumstance so far, what are some possible things God could be trying to teach you?

Now set the paper aside as we look at some other aspects of circumstances.

ATTITUDE TOWARD AUTHORITY

A common cause of adverse circumstances is conflict with authority. Employee with employer. Worker with foreman. Wife with husband. Children with parents. Christian with spiritual leader. Conflict comes from pride: "Only by pride cometh contention" (Proverbs 13:10, KJV). There is something deep within us that resents *any* kind of authority. We want to be independent. We don't want anyone to tell us what to do or how to do it.

Listen in on a conversation in the Lacey home. Randy is thirty-eight and an experienced machinist.

"Can you imagine the nerve of that punk kid?"

"Another run-in with that young engineer?" responded his wife.

"'Young' engineer is hardly the word! 'Ignorant' would be better. I've got fifteen years experience on those machines, and he thinks one course in college and a degree gives him the right to tell me how to do my job?"

"But, Randy, he is in charge of the shop and. . . ."

"I don't care if he owns the place! I refuse to let him tell me how to do my job."

There was a long silence as he hung up his coat. His stomach hurt. He had a headache. Worse yet, he knew his attitude was wrong for a Christian. Then Jan quietly interrupted his thoughts.

"Randy, I wonder if there isn't a pattern to this. Two months ago you were upset because the pastor asked you to change the ushering methods. Three weeks ago you refused to work any overtime. Then you were upset for a week after you got that speeding ticket. It seems as if anytime someone tells you what to do, you get mad."

That really hurt. But as Randy reflected on it, he knew his wife was right: he resented instruction and authority.

Every person is under some kind of authority. We are all under the authority of government and laws. We are under the authority of our employer. We are under the authority of our church. In this context, however, we want to discuss primarily our response and attitude toward authority on the job.

A common evidence of rebellion toward authority is griping and complaining—about the boss, the company, regulations, rules, and myriad other things that arise in the daily routine of work. The complaints may be valid, and you may be encountering unjust treatment. But the attitude of the Christian must be to "do all things without grumbling or disputing; that you may prove yourselves to be blameless and innocent, children of God above reproach in the midst of a crooked and perverse generation, among whom you appear as lights in the world" (Philippians 2:14-15).

"Are you telling me that a Christian is to be totally passive in his job and relationships to authority?" you may ask. By no means. A Christian can discuss the facts of his job and bring grievances to the attention of management. But he is to do so in an orderly fashion within the system of that company. Difficult circumstances normally do not develop from serious grievances, but rather from petty personal irritants. We complain to other employees, to our family and friends. Eventually the complaints affect our performance on the job, and we enter into a conflict with authority. Finally this brings about circumstances that infect every aspect of our lives.

What is your attitude toward authority? Do you resent your foreman, your employer, or your company? How does that affect your attitude each day? Have you seen this resentment create circumstances that bring additional pressure upon you? God has ordained your relationship to that authority. When you rebel, you are really rebelling against

God. This is true whether it is against your employer or the government. If you have difficulty living in one authority structure, you will have difficulty in another. Some people have a history of problems with their supervisors. That is a sure sign of rebellion against God's established authority. Until your attitude is resolved to one that is biblical, you will never have real peace in your job.

> To love those below you is not so difficult. . . . You can love those below you without affecting your pride. Your posture is superior condescension, magnanimous moral conceit. But to love the man above you is different. To love him without flattery or self abasement, to love him without bitterness or resentment, to love him in the midst of conflict and pain: to love the man above you is love's highest hurdle—you cannot get over it alone. You cannot do it without the Cross inside lifting you up.[1]

HOW "BAD" CIRCUMSTANCES DEVELOP

An acquaintance of mine left his job under tense circumstances, and I could not understand why. In my casual contacts with him, he seemed to be fine. Then I had an opportunity to be in some business discussions with him. Almost everything he said had a "barb" in it. Comments or proposals were like a challenge to fight; he simply could not speak in a normal tone that allowed for reasonable discussion. It seemed that he was emotionally involved in every comment.

Some people have a way with words—no matter what they say, they offend. Likewise, some have a knack for getting themselves into difficult circumstances. Often there is a major problem in their personal life, relationships, or home. Every time the situation is discussed, the facts seem to be overwhelmingly on their side as they see it. They are never at fault and always seem to be getting a "bum deal." Though they don't realize it, the circumstances were actually created by them.

Remember the statements earlier about tribulation and pressure? Note that tribulation is not always persecution. Many Christians seem to be perennially in the midst of conflict on their job or with their neighbors or in their church—and they claim to be persecuted. Genuine persecution in our society is unusual: we all undergo some pressure as a result of our faith, but rarely is it persecution. In some instances it may appear that an individual is being persecuted for his faith; but when the facts are known, they reveal he has wrongly related his faith to his coworkers or friends. If you display a belligerent or legalistic manner, for example, you will undoubtedly evoke a hostile response.

In Galatians 6:7 we read that "whatever a man sows, this he will also reap." Though our adverse circumstances are often self-created, this does not change the fact that they exist. But they can teach us a lesson in how to avoid similar circumstances later. Sometimes we are in adverse circumstances because we have sinned: we must live with the consequences of what we have done. Let's be honest with God and with ourselves: when our circumstances are a direct result of our sin, poor judgment, attitudes, or personality, we must admit it. Then we must take steps to correct the cause and to learn what God wants to teach us from the circumstance.

VICTORY, NOT ESCAPE

Often our first response to tough circumstances is to plan a way of escape. We want to avoid bearing the responsibility for our actions. We want relief, not victory.

That philosophy is fine when we deal with sin: we do

want to escape. But we also want the victory of keeping out of similar circumstances in the future.

Let's examine the passage in Philippians 4. Paul said, "I have learned to be content." This is not an automatic response. Contentment is not characteristic of human nature; it is not even natural to a Christian. It is a learned response. You strive for it. You appeal to God in prayer for it. You must learn to live at peace in your circumstances, especially those from which it is impossible to escape.

What does it mean to be content? Certainly it is not some zombielike state of indifference to the world about you. Nor is it wandering through life with a glassy-eyed look and a slightly pious smile—oblivious to the chaos around you. In fact, there may be great pain and difficulty in your circumstances. Contentment means you are persuaded that God is using those circumstances to teach and develop you, and that the circumstances were ordained by Him or at least permitted by Him if they resulted from your sin.

The specific context of Philippians 4:11 concerns money and standard of living. And that relates very closely to work. Our employment provides our finances. Paul said he could get along *with* money or *without* it. He stated that "in any and every circumstance" he had learned the secret of contentment. Paul followed this with one of the more familiar "crutch" verses in the New Testament: "I can do all things through Him who strengthens me" (Philippians 4:13). Note that this "strengthening" and this "doing all things" come in the context of living in the circumstances God provides. You cannot glibly claim verse 13 without coming to grips with being satisfied where God has put you.

How do people try to escape? By leaving the scene? Not always. We knew a student who escaped by sleeping all day and reading all night; he stopped going to all classes and flunked out. Some people try drugs or alcohol. Others immerse themselves in a hobby. Some even try to escape by becoming superactivists in the church. Still others try anything that helps them forget their real problems.

Suppose that you do choose to run and escape. Can it really be done? Probably not. God will pursue you, and you will soon find yourself in another set of circumstances in which He is trying to get your attention and teach you the same thing. Since you cannot escape, why don't you learn to have victory in your present circumstances? In Philippians 4:13 you are promised the strength for that victory. Take advantage of your situation and learn what God has for you in it.

HOW TO HANDLE DIFFICULT CIRCUMSTANCES

Let us not think that there is never a time for voluntarily changing circumstances. In the normal course of finding God's will, there are many times when we definitely *should* change our circumstances. Indeed, circumstances can be an indication of God's directing us toward some other avenue of work, ministry, or location. Chapter 11 focuses on the matter of changing job, location, or career. But here we simply want to develop a process of evaluation of the circumstances we are in. The conclusion of that evaluation may be that we should move to change the circumstances. God frequently used circumstances to lead His people in new directions. Joseph came into Egypt as a result of adverse circumstances. Paul had a witness in Rome because of hostile conditions; he left certain locations of ministry when a situation became impossible. We must be sensitive to understand God's will and to know when a situation is hopeless.

By using the following practical guidelines, you can think through and evaluate your situation and what you should do about it.

1. Write out a few details of your circumstances. Be specific and simple.

2. Describe how the circumstances developed. Jot down a few key items that you can recall in the developing crises. From this you may be able to see where a critical incident occurred that turned good circumstances to bad.

3. What actions on your part may have precipitated some of the circumstances? Can you recall any incident that really aggravated the situation?

4. Was there sin on your part? Were the circumstances self-generated? Be brutally honest with yourself in this. If there was sin, simply bring it to God and confess it. It may be that you will also have to confess this to someone else to correct the problem.

5. What effect have these circumstances had on
   ▶ your family;
   ▶ your spiritual life;
   ▶ your relationships with people?

   If any of these concerns has been drastically affected, you cannot tolerate the status quo for long. Remember that the circumstances may not have caused these to be affected, but simply your *attitude* toward the circumstances.

6. What may God be trying to teach you through these circumstances? What has God taught you so far?

7. Are you willing to stay in the circumstances? This is critical, because God wants you to be neutral in order to find His will. Therefore you need to be willing either to change the circumstances or to live in them.

8. What actions can you take to resolve circumstances? There may be specific things you can do right now. You may need to quit your job, apologize to some-

one, change jobs within your company, change your attitude toward authority, or do what the boss says instead of resisting his direction.

9. If you change the circumstance, would you be avoiding a lesson from God?

10. Write down two or three possible solutions to your adverse circumstances, and then
   ▶ pray about them;
   ▶ seek counsel from someone who is godly and whom you trust;
   ▶ make a decision on what you should do.

11. Take action now! The action may simply be to wait and endure your circumstances patiently. Whatever it is, do it with a clear conscience, knowing God has directed and will bless you.

These steps of evaluation are by no means a "magic potion" that you can apply to find an easy solution. They merely will help you to be honest with yourself and with God. They will give you a basis on which to discern His will.

NOTES: 1. Howard Butt, *The Velvet Covered Brick* (New York: Harper & Row, 1973), page 137.

Chapter Four

WHAT'S THE POINT?

During the nation's economic recession of the mid-seventies, the construction business in Colorado Springs was especially hard hit. Many workers were losing their jobs, and business was slow. Friends of ours in the construction business were caught in the financial pinch. One evening they lingered to talk after a group gathering in our home. Instead of being depressed and despondent, they were happy, outgoing, and expressive of what God was doing in their lives. Their reactions were puzzling to us in view of their circumstances.

They told us, "Just today we sold our snowmobiles, some motorbikes, and other recreational equipment that we thought we just had to have when we had more money. Since we decided to sell these things, we have found that we didn't need them at all. In fact, our family is happier. This has really drawn us together much more than we ever expected. When we had ample money, it seemed as if we could buy anything we wanted for ourselves and for the kids. It just seemed like the right thing to do. But it didn't make us any happier. We have learned a real lesson."

The couple added that having the extra finances was actually a hindrance to them. It caused them to be more materialistic and more inclined to spend money unnecessarily.

THE LURE OF MATERIALISM

Our entire society is plagued by the myth of materialism. Television, radio, and newspapers consistently promote the idea that getting *things* will make a person happy. Even after buying something we have worked hard to get and finding that it does not bring happiness, we still believe that the next little toy will do so. Men want a newer car, a better workshop, fancier tools, a new shotgun, or more stereo equipment. Women want a more modern kitchen, the latest furniture, a bigger house, or a new wardrobe. Children are no longer satisfied with homemade or self-created entertainment and toys, but must have the latest gimmick being advertised on TV or displayed in the stores.

An unfortunate development of this age is that all these things can be acquired immediately without money. The only requirement is a license for indebtedness in the form of a plastic credit card. The sad part of the cycle is that people are never satisfied. What will satisfy? Just a little bit more.

Possessing nice things, however, does not mean a person is materialistic. Having money does not mean a person is greedy. Buying a new car or a new home or a new wardrobe does not mean a person is misusing his money. The key lies in a person's attitude toward material things. What is important to you? What is your objective in life? Is it to make yourself comfortable through material things? One person can have virtually nothing in the way of possessions and yet be materialistic, greedy, and envious. Another person can have a mansion and every possible luxury available and still not be materialistic. It is a matter of heart attitude. In Matthew 6:33 we read, "But seek first His kingdom and His righteousness; and all these things shall be added to you."

Many of us find ourselves grasping for happiness and fulfillment in a vicious circle of acquiring material things. When we finally run head-on into a wall of frustration and ask, "What's the point?" we begin seeking the true objectives of our lives.

GOD'S OBJECTIVES FOR EVERY CHRISTIAN

God did not create the world or man without purpose. Nor does He want life to be lived without direction. He wants us to have objectives for our lives—to know what we are doing and why. The question must be, "Is my objective the right one for me?" To judge rightness and wrongness we need a standard. God does have a discernible objective, clearly taught in the Scriptures. Our objectives must fit God's objectives for us and for the world.

First, God wants every Christian to be growing into the likeness and image of His Son, Jesus Christ. "For whom He foreknew, He also predestined to be conformed to the image of His Son" (Romans 8:29). He wants us to be conformed in every aspect of our lives—thought, action, character, and attitude. This is, of course, a lifelong process.

Second, each Christian is a part of God's instrument for reaching out to the world with the gospel. "Go therefore and make disciples of all the nations, baptizing them in the name of the Father and the Son and the Holy Spirit, teaching them to observe all that I commanded you; and lo, I am with you always, even to the end of the age" (Matthew 28:19-20). We have a direct command from Jesus Christ to share the gospel as widely as possible.

Could anyone ask for two greater objectives? To reach

the world for Christ and to become conformed to the likeness of Christ are goals that challenge every person to his or her greatest potential.

You may think that those objectives sound worthy but very impractical for someone in your circumstances. You would be right if God had not clearly decided how this is to be done. Every Christian in the world *can* have a significant part in sharing the gospel. And every Christian can be growing daily into the image of Christ. This leads us to two of the most crucial sections in this book. We want to examine God's concept of witness and God's concept of discipleship.

CONCEPTS OF DISCIPLESHIP

Everyone expects a baby to act like a baby. But when a five-year-old still acts like a baby and has not grown physically and mentally, there is great concern. It becomes obvious to everyone that something is dreadfully wrong. When a person is a brand new Christian, no one expects him to evidence Christian maturity, but unfortunately many people remain spiritual babies for years.

God intended that we should grow spiritually. He wants us to become mature, committed, and productive members of the Body of Christ. "We are to *grow* up in all aspects into Him, who is the head, even Christ" (Ephesians 4:15). "Like newborn babes, long for the pure milk of the word, that by it you may grow in respect to salvation" (1 Peter 2:2). God wants growth, not stagnation. Growth like this is often called discipleship: we are to be committed disciples of Jesus Christ. The word *disciple* in the Greek simply means "learner." To grow involves both learning and doing. Knowledge alone is not sufficient. We must apply what we learn to our daily living. We must be obedient Christians, not just knowledgeable Christians.

Many factors are involved in discipleship. Walter A. Henrichsen provides an excellent guide to being a disciple in his book *Disciples Are Made—Not Born*.[1] Here is a checklist on some of the basic aspects of discipleship:

▶ A disciple has a regular daily time of reading God's Word and prayer. This is a devotional time, not a study time (Psalm 119, 1 Peter 4:7).

▶ A disciple is actively involved with other Christians in fellowship. This should include involvement in a church and in small groups (Hebrew 10:25).

▶ A disciple studies the Word of God regularly. He is increasing in his knowledge of what the Bible says (2 Timothy 2:15).

▶ A disciple applies the Word to his life. He is making "lordship" decisions—allowing God to control every aspect of his life. He is actively turning away from sin (Proverbs 4:14-15, Luke 9:23).

▶ He is sharing his faith with nonChristians (1 Peter 3:15).

▶ The disciple's place in the home and family is based on Scripture—he or she is fulfilling the scriptural role of training the children in a godly manner (Ephesians 5:22-6:4).

▶ The disciple is developing in his job and work and is relating to it biblically (Ephesians 6:5-9).

This does not require that you be perfect in each of these aspects. It means you are a learner—one who is growing. In a simplified sense, we could say a disciple is one who is in daily fellowship with Christ in His Word and is attempting to put it into practice in his life.

If you try to apply some of the principles from this book in your job and neglect the basics of your personal walk with

God, you will fail. As you grow in discipleship, you will be continually confronted with lordship decisions (putting God first) that will not be easy. Many of those lordship decisions will be related to your work. For example, you may be asked to do something unethical or dishonest; our response is a lordship decision. Or, there may be much opportunity for overtime and extra pay; but if you need to spend more time with your family or in Christian ministry, it is a lordship decision to forgo the extra money. If those first points of discipleship are actively experienced in your life, you will have the foundation you need to respond properly in each lordship decision.

Is Christ Lord of your life now? Are there aspects that you are knowingly withholding from Him? If there are, settle them with God now. Have you committed your job to God? You may have to do that before much of this book makes sense to you. In many ways discipleship precedes witness. Without discipleship our witness becomes hypocritical. And no one likes a hypocrite—especially nonChristians.

Can anyone be a true disciple without having a biblical relationship to his job? The growing disciple knows that God has put him where he is and wants him to enjoy what he is doing. God has put him there for the purpose of reaching out to the lost. Are you a disciple in your job?[2]

SETTING OBJECTIVES THAT WORK

Every decision we make is based on one of the following:

Habit. No premeditation is involved with habits. We do a certain thing because we have done it before. The habit can be either bad or good, can serve us or work against us.

Urgency and fear. We do some things because of the consequences of not doing them. We pay certain bills promptly and put off others. We get to work on time, but not to church on time.

Desire. Some things we do because we simply enjoy doing them. The basis may be lust; it may have nothing to do with importance or need. This can be an overwhelming motivation and at times even irrational.

Expediency. We may do something, not because we want to or because it is the best action, but simply because we want to achieve a certain goal. People cheat because it is the easiest way to attain the objective. Lies are often a result of expediency. This motivation is the outworking of the philosophy that the end justifies the means.

Chosen direction. We choose some actions, either on our own, by God's direction, or by the direction of someone else. These decisions are based upon correct objectives and priorities. We know why we do them, and we have made a conscious choice about them.

The first four motivations do not require deliberation—they just happen. Only the fifth is a deliberate option. At times each of these has a proper place: we need not ponder the merits of brushing our teeth; we do not need to make a decision whether to eat at mealtime; we feel free to do some things from desire, such as recreation; taking short-cuts may be wise when moral or legal conflicts are not involved. But we want to operate our lives on a more substantial basis than the first four motivations alone provide. We want to base our lives on objectives that relate to God's goals for us. We want to govern our lives by personal decision and choice.

Let's define an objective: *It is a specific goal to be reached at the end of a considered period of time.*

▶ To read the Bible through in one year.
▶ To finish a job-related correspondence course by September 1.
▶ To take my son on two camping trips this year.

Are these objectives? Only in a limited sense. They are more accurately viewed as activities that we might do to reach some objectives. Let's try again:

> ▶ To grow in my knowledge of the Scriptures by
>> reading the Bible through in one year;
>> studying the books of John and Galatians this year.
> ▶ To increase my proficiency on the job in regard to supervising by
>> completing a supervisors' correspondence course by July 31;
>> praying daily for the men I supervise.
> ▶ To deepen my relationship with my son this year by
>> taking him on two camping trips;
>> going to at least four of his team's basketball games.

Do you see the difference? The camping trip is not crucial. My relationship with my son is the important thing.

There are two kinds of objectives:

> ▶ Short range (weeks or months to two years);
> ▶ Long range (two years and beyond).

There are four categories of objectives:

> ▶ Personal-spiritual (your relationship to God);
> ▶ Family;
> ▶ Job;
> ▶ Ministry (outwardly directed spiritual activities such as church, Bible studies, witnessing).

Are these in order of priority? In general, yes. But in practice they must blend and balance such that at any one point any of the four could be taking priority in terms of time. In my twenties, as I was just seeing the spiritual and ministry elements of my life grow to prominence in my thinking, I placed ministry above my job. My friend and fellow faculty member at the United States Air Force Academy, Dr. Dick Warren, challenged my thinking on this, insisting that job must precede ministry. I didn't agree at the time. However, later I came to see that he was right, because my job is an integral part of my ministry.

Why do we need objectives at all? Because most of us live in a frenzy of "good" activities without even asking, "Why am I doing this?"

John typifies an activist in our church. He was involved in everything—taught Sunday school, served on the board, attended every meeting, held evangelistic Bible studies in his home, and participated in special projects. Finally his body ran down. He lost sleep and became ineffective at work, and his family rebelled.

"What do you think is your main objective in life, John?"

"Well, that's a hard question. I guess to become a man of God, to be a good father, and to do my part in sharing Christ with the unsaved."

"Those are really good objectives. Let's take the first one. Are you doing personal Bible study?"

"Uh, not really. I just use the teaching manual for Sunday school and follow a prepared course in the evangelistic study."

"How's your prayer time?"

"Ouch! Pretty slim."

"Are you doing anything that would help you become a man of God?"

"Let's see. . . ."

"John, it's obvious that your objective is *not* to be a man of God. That's a pipe dream!''

John had no real objectives. Notice that he did not even mention his job. It is all too easy to be busy "doing" with no purpose except to try to fulfill other people's expectations.

Another important factor is priorities. Priorities determine what we do first, second, or not at all when we have a choice. They are based on our objectives. We cannot have priorities without implying some objectives. But we will discuss priorities later. Let's get specific and practical on objectives now.

With a blank piece of paper before you, take a moment to ask God to help you set some realistic objectives for your life.

1. Quickly jot down several things you would like to see happen in your life, family, and job in the next ten years. Don't linger on this—just write some thoughts (e.g., be a good husband, change careers, have a significant prayer life). As you write short-term objectives, you can see if they fit any of these ten-year goals. Establish and complete short-term goals for several months before trying to settle on specific long-term ones.

2. Let's brainstorm on some short-range objectives. Think in terms of one to three months. Divide your page under headings of the four categories (personal-spiritual, family, job, and ministry). Start jotting down random ideas on possible objectives for your life; these may reflect your known needs, wants, or hopes. Place them in the proper categories. Don't ponder too much, but write down your wildest (or most insignificant) thoughts. Taken only ten or fifteen minutes for this list; you can revise it later. Try to put at least five or six things in each category.

3. Beside each item put a code to show if it is an objective (OB) or activity (A). (See example on page 57.)

PERSONAL-SPIRITUAL

OB Develop a consistent
    devotional life.
A Pray ten minutes daily.

A _____

OB _____

FAMILY

A Pray with my wife.
OB Develop a deeper relation-
    ship with my son.

OB _____

A _____

JOB

A Get to work on time.
OB Have a better testimony
    at work.
OB Do better work.

A _____

OB _____

MINISTRY

OB Witness to my neighbors.
A Ask our next-door neigh-
    bor for dinner.
OB Improve teaching in Sun-
    day school.

A _____

4. Carefully select one objective (and only one) that you consider the most important in each category. List these four items on a separate sheet of paper.

5. This is the crucial stage. For each of the four objectives, write down *one* activity you can do in the next month to help achieve that goal. Make each activity simple, realistic, and workable. For instance, if your goal is to develop your prayer life, do not prescribe an activity of praying one hour a day for thirty days: you would certainly fail. Rather, set a goal of praying five minutes a day, at least five days each week. If your objective is to do better work in your job, don't list an activity of increasing your production 100 percent; rather, seek to correct one aspect in which you know you have been lax in the production system.

6. Now, from the four categories, choose the best one to begin tomorrow. After one week, select another category and work on the two together for another week. In the third week, add a third activity. Do the three for a week, and then add the fourth. In other words, do not attempt to achieve

all your objectives at once, but gradually increase your efforts.

7. When each activity has been in effect for a month, evaluate your progress. Now you can make adjustments. Your activities should develop into good habits and attitudes so they no longer take great conscious effort.

8. As you succeed in setting short-term objectives and activities, you can become more ambitious and go for longer times or more significant objectives. Return to your original list and determine the next most important objective in each category. You may also want to continue adding new ideas to this list.

The key: Keep it simple. Do not try to do everything at once. Be realistic and discipline yourself to do what you set out to accomplish. "Desire realized is sweet to the soul" (Proverbs 13:19).

A warning: Don't expect miracles. This is just a tool to help you put meaning and direction into your life. Nothing can replace the daily communication with God in which you find His will for you for the day. But if you have prayed about your objectives, the two will likely coincide.

9. This is more difficult. Over a period of three months, *eliminate* one activity that does not fit any of your objectives. You cannot keep adding activities to an already full schedule without eliminating something.

10. Say no to at least one activity in which you are asked to participate that does not contribute to your objective. Get into the habit of being selective in the responsibilities you take on. Never be afraid to say no.

Now you have a start. Work at it until you feel comfortable with setting objectives (but not too comfortable, for a little pressure is helpful).

A final suggestion to keep you "honest": *Have someone check up on you!*

TIME AND PRIORITIES

"Which is more valuable—time or money?" asked the young student.

"Ask any rich old man," replied the millionaire.

Time presses us. It frustrates us. It disappears. There never seems to be enough. Even when we use it well, we wonder if it could have been used better. Time spent with no objective is discouraging. If we have no clear objectives, life is absurd.

> We go, and keep on going,
> Until the object of the game
> Seems to be
> To go and keep on going.
>
> We do, and keep on doing,
> Until we do
> Without knowing—without feeling.
>
> Is there no time to stop and reflect?
> Is there no time to stop?
> Is there no time?
>
> If we stopped, would we keep on going?
> If we reflected, would we keep doing
> What we do?
>
> For what we have done
> And where we have gone
> Is dissolved into oblivion
> Or strung on the meaningless chain
> Or half-remembered this and that
> If there is no reflection.

In all our doing have we done anything?
In all our going have we been anywhere?
—*Author unknown*

Priorities without objectives are meaningless. Objectives without priorities are futile. Both require time for fulfillment.

Let us be practical. Most of our time is already taken by our job or other mandatory responsibilities. We have only a limited amount over which we have control—our *discretionary* time. How much is there? On working days:

8 hours	work
½ hour	lunch
1 hour	transportation
1 hour	two other meals (breakfast, dinner)
8 hours	sleep
1 hour	miscellaneous mandatory items
———	
19½ hours	

This leaves about four and one-half hours per working day for us to use as we desire—or twenty-two and one-half hours each work week. Now assume there are eight hours of discretionary time on Saturday and six on Sunday (excluding church), for a total of thirty-six and one-half hours per week. Add a few household projects, shopping, preparing meals, taking the children to various activities, and some other "necessities," and we are down to about twenty-four hours. Not much left of the original 168 hours, is there? These twenty-four hours are available to fulfill our objectives other than job goals. But notice: that is equivalent to three full working days, or sixty percent of the time we put into our jobs!

All we have to do to blow it all is to throw in a few

meaningless activities—an hour a day of TV, or one meeting that does not meet our objectives—and we have just destroyed half of our discretionary time. We must have priorities, or we will just muddle through life "hoping it will all work out."

As a young Air Force lieutenant, I was involved in many activities on the base. I taught a high school class, ran the youth program, was chairman of the junior officers' council, sang in a choral society, played sports, led a Bible study, maintained a hi-fi and electronics hobby, and held a demanding round-the-clock job. I rarely saw my son. I left my wife with the entire home responsibility. I was not wandering; I was running at top speed—in every direction at once, with no objectives and no explicit priorities. My wife tried to slow me down, but I would not listen. I had to run into a wall to learn the lesson: Listen to your wife. Wives often are more perceptive than husbands in seeing the outcome of our activity cycle, especially as it relates to the children.

I finally ended up flat on my back from physical exhaustion. God got my attention, and I vowed to set my objectives and live by priorities. It was a turning point in my life.

A very basic list of priorities includes:

▶ your personal walk with God,
▶ your family,
▶ your job,
▶ your ministry.

Does that mean that if there is a family problem, you don't go to work that day? Or if you have not had a "quiet time" that day, does it mean that you do not lead a Bible study? No. It means that over a period of days or weeks, the priorities are kept. There may be brief periods when one aspect (such as the job) will jump ahead of the others for a time and we will concentrate on it almost totally.

Specifically, your priorities should come from your objectives. If an objective involves time with the family, then it must take a clear priority in the week. Daily or weekly, jot down your priorities. It sounds simple. It is. And it works. Remember that you are working with those thirty-six and one-half discretionary hours.

How do you go about scheduling your time to get everything done? This is the easiest process of all. The 3 x 5 card is the best time-management tool since the clock. On one side of the card, write your priorities for the week; on the other side, keep a running "do list" for each day of the week. Also, keep a list of small or quick items that you can do in a three-minute period or on the backstroke. (See the following example.)

FRONT SIDE

Do
  Mow lawn
4. Finish Bible study lesson by
   Wednesday
1. Work on testimony (2
   hours)
   Write the Smiths
2. Talk to daughter about
   schoolwork
3. Help son with math

Call/Misc.
1. Get gas for car
2. Call Johnsons 555-1173
3. Call spouse (during coffee
   break)

BACK SIDE

Priorities
1. Personal quiet time (15 min.)
2. Talk with spouse 15 min.
   daily and be available to the
   children
3. Finish yard work
4. Work on my written personal testimony

After making the "do list," order the activities according to priority. Some must be done simply from urgency, but if that becomes the norm, you are not adequately planning ahead.

We can follow the same procedure at work if we have a kind of job in which we have options on our time.

To demonstrate the need for scheduling and planning, keep a record for a week of how you use your "off the job" time. Better yet, reflect on last week and write down how each evening and the weekend were used. What percentage of time was wasted?

A final suggestion: Because most of us work better with some regularity or habit, try to set up some kind of schedule. Do not try to do it by the minute, but in general terms. For example:

Monday	Open
Tuesday	Personal Bible study
Wednesday	Family night
Thursday	Group Bible study
Friday	Open for entertaining
Saturday	Morning: Study and personal projects
	Afternoon: Shopping and household projects
	Evening: Open
Sunday	Morning: Church
	Afternoon: Plan week, extra time in prayer, special time with one of the children.

From this general schedule, plan the specifics for each week. Plan for interruptions and broken schedules by leaving some open or overflow time: you will need it. In planning like this, some worry about being "too organized" or "inflexible." Frankly, that problem is rare.

The greatest hindrances to living an ordered life are:

▶Time wasters (such as television or excessive sports or hobbies),
▶Laziness,
▶No plan or goal.

Some Hints for Better Use of Time

Often the small requests for our time and the "little things" ruin our plans and schedules. In the same manner, little ideas can pay great dividends. Here are some ideas that have helped us greatly:

▶Think of evenings in two blocks of time, 6 to 8 and 8 to 10.
▶Keep something with you to work on when you are in lines or waiting (Scripture memory, your "do-list," reading, etc.).
▶Keep a flexible mind-set. Your plans will never work just as you desire.
▶Don't become upset when people invade your plans.
▶Try to *always* have three nights per week at home.
▶Get adequate sleep, rest, and exercise.[3]

Use Your Saturday for Maximum Accomplishment

For most people Saturday is a wasted day. We rise later, putter around the house, read the paper, have an extra cup of coffee, run a few errands, watch part of a ball game, and soon it's gone—with little accomplished. The one day over which you have complete control—wasted. We should plan our Saturdays well and not let them just slip away. These guidelines may prove helpful:

▶Get up at a reasonably early hour and have a *good* devotional time. It is the one unhurried time you can count on in the week.

▶Use the morning for study, Sunday school lesson preparation, or preparation for next week's activities.

▶If you have a large project (e.g., painting or building), plan ahead, get the materials beforehand, and work hard at it. It is often best to do this in the afternoon, but on hot days start earlier.

▶Avoid little projects and errands. Use the time just before the evening meal on workdays to do these.

▶Give your wife a couple of hours to herself. You can take care of the children (and not just while she does the shopping).

▶Avoid the big time trap of a four-hour game or movie on TV. This is not always wrong, but note that it is about fifteen percent of your free time. Don't waste it (though some large projects permit having a radio or television nearby).

▶Plan your Saturday nights a month ahead. Make one of them an evening out with your mate. Use another to have a couple in. Another should include a family activity. Spend at least one of them at home. (Again, don't make TV the center of your home life; limit its use for *all* the family.)

Separate Your Work and Life

When a job is distasteful and unfulfilling, we tend to segregate it from the rest of life. It becomes like a bad habit or a chronic pain—we just try our best to ignore it. We live for the evening or the weekend. If you pass forty hours each week with that attitude, you waste twenty-five percent of your total life and forty percent of your waking hours. What a tragedy to spend that much of your time in a depressing, disagreeable activity! Your attitude must contribute to your self-esteem, your ministry to others, and your total life. Remember that God gave you that job to reach people—not just to put bread on the table. Integrate your job into your life and stop living in two worlds.

NOTES: 1. See Walter A. Henrichsen, *Disciples Are Made—Not Born* (Wheaton, Ill.: Victor Books/Scripture Press, 1974).

2. For further reference, see Jerry White, *Honesty, Morality, and Conscience* (Colorado Springs, Colo.: NavPress, 1979), and *Choosing Plan A in a Plan B World* (Colorado Springs, Colo.: NavPress, 1987).

3. See Archibald Hart, *Adrenaline and Stress* (Waco, Tex.: Word, Inc., 1986).

Chapter Five

FULFILLMENT— THE ILLUSIVE GOAL

G od never intended that men and women find their fulfillment in their work, no matter how much they enjoy it or how important it is. Engineers, plumbers, machinists, doctors, pastors, social workers, homemakers, teachers, and businessmen will all encounter great disappointment if they seek to find fulfillment in their work. Work is but one part of life—a big part, but only one. The illusive life value, fulfillment, comes from the whole of life, not just work. At times work may dominate, but family, health, emotional well-being, spiritual condition, and many other factors make up the total.

It would be easy to declare that fulfillment is found only in one's relationship to Jesus Christ and personal spiritual walk. Though this is technically true, it gives small comfort to the average Christian trapped in the trenches of real life where "spiritual sounding" answers irritate more than help.

Our focus in this study is your job, so we need to examine the part it plays in fulfillment. The face of the workplace is changing rapidly as the technological revolution continues. Midlevel managers are disappearing. Some skills are disappearing completely. Analysts say that "high-touch" must accompany our new "high-tech" environment, which speaks to the desire for the human dimensions of work.

The decrease of company loyalty and stability change the view of a career drastically. For instance, men in their sixties generally have had one career and two jobs. The generation of those in their forties will experience two careers and three to five jobs. The next generation will have three careers and five to seven jobs. Thus, some of the factors in the past that favored a significant part of fulfillment—stability, loyalty, and even a specific career skill—simply are not present.

Does that mean we should abandon finding *any* fulfillment in the job? No! It does mean that we must adjust to the reality of today's work *and* learn the components of fulfillment for ourselves.

A MEASURE OF FULFILLMENT

Certainly everyone wants a good measure of fulfillment in his or her job. But can you know when you are fulfilled? Is it when you are getting enough money? When you are free from conflict or problems on the job? When you have job security? When you feel "good" and are happy about your circumstances?

It is not just one of these things, nor is it all of them combined. We can be totally fulfilled in the midst of conflict and problems. Contribution brings fulfillment even when pay and other benefits are small. We would deny our humanity to expect total, irrevocable fulfillment. Fulfillment is dynamic and changing. We must look at it like climate, not the weather: weather is the daily situation of varying conditions; climate is the average weather in a given area. Look at the average fulfillment over a period of time.

Measuring fulfillment is difficult. In fact, job fulfillment cannot be measured in terms of the job alone. It *must* be measured in concert with your personal and family satisfaction and circumstances. The following questions provide an approximate gauge for job fulfillment:

1. To the best of your understanding, do you have a vital daily walk with Christ? (Personal devotions, obedience in major areas of your life.)   ____

2. Do you function in your family according to the pattern of Scripture? (Husband and wife fulfilling biblical roles, family guided on a spiritual basis in love and unity.)   ____

3. Are you basically happy with your job?   ____

4. Do you do your best on the job?   ____

5. Have you witnessed to someone on your job in the last year?   ____

6. Has it been at least six months since you sincerely contemplated quitting your job?   ____

7. Do you feel the job you are doing is worthwhile?   ____

8. Do you feel the job adequately makes use of your abilities?   ____

9. Do you go to work daily with ease of mind? (As opposed to dreading it or focusing mostly on the weekend.)   ____

10. Does your job meet the primary financial needs of your family?   ____

Clearly there is no "right" score. But if you answered no to question 1 or 2, you probably do not find peace in your job. If you responded yes to five or more of the remaining, you are reasonably fulfilled in your job now.

Before we set forth a few suggestions for increasing job fulfillment, let's return to our initial statement. God does not intend that every person be fulfilled in his job.

Is it sin not to be fulfilled? Biblically the answer must be no. God does not promise or command job fulfillment. We must be *content* in our circumstances, but we might not experience *fulfillment*. The Bible does not say directly that God does not expect a person to be fulfilled in the job, but this is derived inductively from passages like Colossians 3:22-23. This statement was specifically addressed to slaves: they were to work heartily as to the Lord. Being a slave was not a fulfilling job, but one was to be content as a Christian. In prison, Joseph was not fulfilled, but he was content (Genesis 39-41). Does God expect a man who spends his days in a coal mine breathing dust and laboring hard to say he wants to do this more than anything else? Working on an assembly line, putting the same part on a car, or punching out the same machine part every day may not be your idea of a perfect job. Many jobs are difficult, offer little recognition, and allow no prospects of promotion. In such circumstances we must accept God's sovereignty in placing us where we are. Biblical fulfillment is found, not only on the job, but in the interrelationship of personal activities, family ties, and work. Many jobs serve the family by providing for them. In fact, Christians will rarely find real fulfillment only in a job.

But is it legitimate to strive for fulfillment? Yes, it is. Here are five key steps to work on:

1. Acknowledge that God has placed you in your job and thank Him for it.
2. Do the best work you can in your job, both in attitude and action.
3. Do whatever is necessary to resolve personal conflicts with coworkers even if it means losing face.

4. Actively seek and take advantage of opportunities
   to witness to those with whom you work.
5. Begin a program of development to improve or
   change jobs if this is within your abilities and
   desires.

These are simply suggestions, but effective when you put
them into practice.

FACTORS OF CONTENTMENT IN YOUR WORK

Though God does not promise fulfillment in our work, He
does promise contentment. Some may have a problem with
the word "contentment" since it sounds so soft, so passive,
so idealistic.

Consider instead "confident contentment"—the sure
knowledge that you are where God wants you at this time,
coupled with drive, desire, and motivation to be your best
for Him. It is not passive acceptance, but active involvement—
whether in good circumstances or bad.

We propose that three elements pave the way for biblical contentment in work—contribution, relationships, and
attitude.

Meaningful Contribution

Everyone wants to know that his life and work possess some
meaning, and that he is not just a cog in some meaningless
wheel of activity. Everyone wants his job to be a worthwhile
task. People need to sense that they are making a meaningful
contribution both to society and to God's Kingdom.

In the earlier discussion on society, we concluded that
society is not evil, but is planned by God as an environment
in which people live, work, and play. It is God's plan for the
sustenance of His creation. It is easy to see how a physician or

worker who produces food contributes. But how does one who designs or builds plastic toys that have a two-hour life expectancy in the hands of a spirited child view contribution? Or a producer of bubble gum? Or trinkets to decorate a car's rear-view mirror? None of these items are truly necessary for the preservation or enlightenment of mankind. Yet each item fits into the economic structure of a nation, giving jobs and economic development. The production facilities in a city provide employment, a context for living for families, and natural contact with nonChristians. The work to produce such a product may not "feel" satisfying, yet the task is a meaningful contribution to the society.

Then we all need to know that we are making a contribution to the Kingdom of God. Again, we return to the concept of being salt and light in society. Christians are placed by God in their work and neighborhood to provide a credible witness for Christ. If there is no attempt to make Christ known nor a desire on your part to do so, we would propose that fulfillment is little more than a dream. A purpose from God gives meaning and direction to even the most mundane of activities.

There is also a contribution to other believers—serving, teaching, leading—which also gives motivation and fulfillment in our lives. We need the knowledge that we are making a contribution to these people.

Together, these contributions make up one part of the goal of fulfillment. Lacking a clear sense of contribution, life lapses into a sense of meaninglessness. In fact, we become little different from nonChristians seeking to find meaning in worldly pursuits.

Relationships
Most people find their greatest job stress not in the work itself, but in the relationships with people at work. Conflict,

tensions, disagreement, unjust treatment, and irritating personalities are but a few of the relational problems that plague us at work. Yet they are unrelentingly present. Where there are people, there will be problems. Learning how to develop good interpersonal relationships will unlock a gold mine of opportunity for personal success as well as personal fulfillment. We have discovered five obstacles to overcome in developing good relationships in the workplace.

1. The first obstacle is *personal competition*. If we attempt to "beat someone out," "cut his throat," or "get his job" it is highly unlikely that a good personal relationship will develop! Yet, competition is a necessity of modern commerce. It is also a fact of life in the workplace. People compete for jobs, status, money, and promotions. But *how* they compete determines the relationship. We must guard our competitive drives to keep them from becoming vindictive, scheming, or unethical.

2. The next obstacle is *ambition* and *ability*. We will discuss this fully in Chapter 7. Outwardly ambitious people often earn a reputation for "getting ahead, no matter what" and offend many of their coworkers in the process. The person with little or no ambition also creates relational problems by not holding up his part of the workload or losing the respect of others.

The evaluation and use of ability is a more subtle matter. Romans 12:3 instructs each of us "not to think more highly of himself than he ought to think; but to think so as to have sound judgment." We are not to overestimate or underestimate our abilities. The greatest relational danger in the workplace is to overestimate or overstate our abilities. For those who know us well, it ruins our credibility. In other cases, it can come across as pride. We need to use our abilities in an unselfish, focused way, readily admitting when we cannot do a particular task.

3. Perhaps the most difficult of all relational problems centers on the theme of *authority*. In Chapter 3 we discussed the effects of our attitudes toward authority. Our attitude strongly affects our relationships. No one likes authority. No one likes to be told what to do. Whether it is a child telling us to hold him, a spouse asking for help with the household work, or a boss directing our tasks, most people experience an inner rebellion resisting the request. At work, in the church, or at home, authority is almost universally resisted— at least inwardly. Then this resistance causes conflict and relational problems. There are four authorities that every believer must learn to accept and live with, or he simply will not be a happy, fulfilled person.

First is the authority of the *employer*. The boss is the boss regardless of how he gained that position or whether he is just or fair. Certainly employers have legal and moral limits on their authority. When they function within those limits, we are obligated to respond—in good spirits. Legitimate grievances do develop in every job. Those should be handled with sensitivity and according to legal or company procedures. Ephesians 6:5,9 gives both employees and employers commands for proper conduct.

Second is the authority of the *government*. Regardless of the country, that government is ordained by God (Romans 13:1). Each will have, to a greater or lesser degree, laws and actions that are not biblical or just. But the majority of the laws are for the good of the people to live an ordered and safe life. Becoming upset and angry about them does little more than make you a hard person to get along with.

Governmental laws exist at two primary levels—national and local. Nationally we live under laws of taxation, work rules, and business rules. Locally, we learn to live with speed limits, property zoning regulations, educational systems, and city or neighborhood rules. Both authorities affect us greatly. We must learn to live peaceably under these authorities. When we do not, our spirits become agitated and bitter. These feelings then overshadow most of our relationships.

Third, we live in a *family* authority structure. Husbands and wives each experience authority. Children live in this authority structure—and often rebel against it. We need to bring our family into a biblical authority structure. What is learned and practiced there will extend to our relationships to authority in all other aspects of life.

Finally, there is *spiritual* authority. The Bible speaks of spiritual leaders who possess and exercise spiritual authority. Because it is seldom practiced, the church is weakened and anemic. This is not the context to discuss spiritual authority among believers, but it is a needed discussion. Are you under anyone's authority spiritually? Or are you a spiritual loner, independent and not spiritually accountable to anyone? If so, you will always struggle against any kind of authority.

Remember that no authority is complete or absolute except God's authority. Therefore, all these authorities are limited. Also, all authorities are, and most likely will be, misused or abused.

But that does not make the authority illegitimate. We do not outlaw cars because some people get killed in them, or electricity because people are electrocuted. Rather, we control them and use them as they were intended. So we do the same with authority—use it as God intended.

4. The next means of enhancing relationships is *serving*. Christ was a servant, and He came to serve (Matthew 20:25-28). A servant is always welcome. If you have as your heart motive or goal to serve your boss, your spouse, your children, your coworkers, and your subordinates, you will find that you enter an entirely new realm of interpersonal relationships—all for the better. Also, you will be taken

advantage of at times, that is, expected to serve. Jesus was also taken advantage of, so we should not expect less. Learn to serve and you will begin building bridges of relationships.

5. Finally, relational problems are greatly increased by a *lack of communication.* Learn to ask good questions to find out what is expected of you. Learn to speak up when you don't understand what is expected of you. Learn to surface issues of disagreement before they escalate to the explosive stage. These steps are vital in relationships on the job. Silence is not golden when it comes to job relationships.

People of certain personalities find communication very difficult. They may express themselves in a confrontive or argumentative manner. Or they may find it difficult to admit that they need help. If you are one of these, you can be helped and you can improve, but only if you recognize the problem and seek help.

Communication is key to understanding, and understanding is key to good relationships.

Attitude

When you or your spouse comes home from work, how long does it take to discover his or her attitude? One minute? Ten seconds? It is almost immediate. The frown, tone of voice, body posture, silence all indicate one's attitude. It is almost impossible to hide.

Who hasn't heard the statement, "Don't go near the boss today. She got up on the wrong side of the bed." We are all like that. We have bad days. But what if a poor attitude prevails in most of our days? Then no one will choose to be near us. Philippians 2:5 says, "Have this attitude in you which was also in Christ Jesus." That was not an attitude of complaining and bitterness, but an attitude of humility and serving.

Your attitude will build or break your relationships. No

one wants to be near a person who is constantly irritable or irritating. Your attitude is a reflection of your mind-set toward your work. You will never enjoy your work if you harbor attitudes of resentment, bitterness, hatred, griping, or demandingness. There are always things to complain about. But we can choose whether or not to complain. We can choose—*decide*—to have a good attitude, even in the midst of stretching circumstances.

Remember, other people can see

▶ how you work,
▶ how you talk,
▶ your attitude.

Don't let the windows of your life get clouded and dirty.

ARE LABORING JOBS DEMEANING?

"My brethren, do not hold your faith in our glorious Lord Jesus Christ with an attitude of personal favoritism. For if a man comes into your assembly with a gold ring and dressed in fine clothes, and there also comes in a poor man in dirty clothes, and you pay special attention to the one who is wearing the fine clothes, and say, 'You sit here in a good place,' and you say to the poor man, 'You stand over there, or sit down by my footstool,' have you not made distinctions among yourselves, and become judges with evil motives?" (James 2:1-4).

Little has changed in the nineteen centuries since those words were written. In Christian circles there is still a strong tendency to value or give honor to the person of position or wealth. When describing members of a group or church you often hear of "Dr. Jones" or "Mr. Johnson, the president of the firm" or "Colonel Jackson." Seldom is it expressed as

"Mr. Williams, the carpenter" (unless he owns a business) or "Mr. Benton, the mechanic." Perhaps without really meaning to, we place extra value on those who have position or wealth or marks of notable success.

The truth is, churches, neighborhoods, and social groups *do* divide along class, social, and economic lines. If a church is large, it tends to subdivide into smaller, homogeneous groups. Usually a person finds himself in the social or economic group directly related to his kind of job. Is this wrong? Are not all Christians to be equal in the Body of Christ? Yes, but remember that society is not Christian and that God intends for us to reach out to all society.

If every person who became a Christian were suddenly famous or rich, would that person continue to live in an old house, eat the same food, and drive the same car? Or would he rent or buy a nicer house, wear better clothes, and even change social associations? Most would do the latter. Recall the earlier discussion on concepts of witness: God's objective is to influence and reach all segments of the community. Therefore He has sovereignly placed Christians in every level of society, with different abilities and social and economic standing—to be witnesses.

Laboring and Unskilled Jobs

There is no truly "unskilled" job: every task involves skill. Many people could not endure a job requiring great physical strength or stamina; some professionally trained persons are totally incompetent when it comes to manual skills.

I read recently of a man who bought a new gadget—unassembled, of course. After reading and rereading the instructions, he could not understand how to put it together. Finally he sought the help of an old handyman who was working in the backyard. The old fellow picked up the pieces, studied them, and then began assembling the gadget.

In a short time he had it all put together.

"That's amazing!" said the man. "And you did it without even looking at the instructions!"

"Fact is," said the handyman, "I can't read. And when a fellow can't read, he's got to think."[1]

Jobs do require different degrees of mechanical skill, physical strength, and mental or academic ability. Wages are generally related to the supply of people who can do a particular job and the public demand for the service or product. Consider who would be missed most quickly: lawyers, engineers, and dentists; or garbage collectors, store clerks, and truckdrivers. Certainly the latter would be missed more quickly, but the former probably earn more money.

In Scripture, great honor is bestowed on persons with mechanical skills. The farmer or laborer who is diligent and faithful is exalted. Gideon was a farmer. Peter was a fisherman. God uses spiritual men regardless of their wealth or position. "For consider your calling, brethren, that there were not many wise according to the flesh, not many mighty, not many noble [whom God chose]" (1 Corinthians 1:26).

God will certainly use the talented and wise person, but such a one is often too proud to open himself up to God. In history we see that many times God has used people of common background and ordinary occupations.

Are laboring or unskilled jobs demeaning? The answer is a resounding no! It is no biblically. It is no in terms of value to society. It is no in regard to human worth. It is no in the eyes of law. It is yes only in the warped value system of a materially corrupt society. A person's value is not in what he *does*, but in who he *is*.

Does this mean that a person should not attempt to gain more skills or education to get a higher-paying job? Should he placidly accept his lot in life and not try to change? Of course not. But it means that if his ability or training is such that change is unlikely or impossible, he must not be bitter against God for his station in life. God has placed him there for a specific purpose and clearly promises him peace and great contentment in his circumstances.

Recognition of Personal Ability

Are people really equal? Yes, they are of equal worth in God's sight. But they are not equal in ability or attainment. People have widely varied abilities, manual skills, intellectual capacities, and spiritual gifts. "We have gifts that *differ* according to the grace given to us," we read in Romans 12:6. Each of us is different and unique in God's sight. We must recognize that some are more intelligent or more skillful. It is not a matter of "better or worse," just difference.

Recognize also that people with essentially equal ability will have different levels of attainment. Even among David's mighty men, Benaiah "was honored among the thirty, but he *did not attain* to the three" (1 Chronicles 11:25). God simply wants each one to use to the fullest the abilities He has given. The end result is up to Him.

It is easy to be jealous of another Christian who has great gifts and abilities. And that Christian may be jealous of someone else. We read earlier, "Where jealousy and selfish ambition exist, there is disorder and every evil thing" (James 3:16). This is another form of coveting what belongs to another, and it is sin.

What about equality in the Christian community? Everyone must be treated as equal in value, and we must not show preference to any (James 2:1-4). But even in this there are differing gifts and abilities to fulfill the total functioning of the Body of Christ. We *must* recognize these differences. Not everyone is a leader, not everyone can sing, not everyone can teach. Assuming that the spiritual qualifications of

1 Timothy 3 are met, not every person is qualified for every responsibility or office in the church. One who cannot balance his own checkbook or prepare a budget for his family should not be church treasurer. A person who effectively teaches a class of eight may not be able to teach a class of fifty.

We need to recognize abilities and help people find their most productive place in the Body of Christ. Remember, too, that we all change: God changes us as we grow. We can learn new skills and develop our gifts and abilities, so we must never restrict ourselves or others with a "permanent" evaluation.

A Proper Self-Image

Many Christians have a distorted view of themselves. They do not see themselves as others see them, nor do they see themselves as God sees them. In some respects they feel inferior; in some, superior. "I say to every man among you not to think more highly of himself than he ought to think; but to think so as to have sound judgment" (Romans 2:3). The Phillips version says, "Try to have a sane estimate of your capabilities." And in the Living Bible, "Be honest in your estimate of yourselves."

What we seek is truth about ourselves. But truth often hurts. We would rather live in a dream world imagining that we are this or that. One of the marks of a mature Christian is that he welcomes truth in every aspect of life; he becomes more truthful to and about himself. A proper self-image is not an inflated ego, nor is it an attitude of worthlessness. It is a growing knowledge of gifts and abilities and a spirit of thanksgiving that God has made you as you are. It is not an "I-guess-that's-the-way-I-am" attitude that suppresses change and hinders growth. It is a realistic evaluation that forms a basis for change and growth.

Here are some ideas for developing a good self-image

and a "sane estimate" of your attitudes:

1. Ask God to enable you to see the abilities and gifts He has given you and to be thankful for them.
2. List your strengths, weaknesses, and abilities as you know them. (Consider in what ways God has blessed you in the past.)
3. Ask two or three close friends, and possibly your employer, to evaluate you in these aspects.
4. When you feel you have clearly identified a particular strength, weakness, or ability, consciously thank God for what you have *and* for what you do not have.
5. Begin to use and develop your strengths and abilities.
6. Begin to withdraw from activities or tasks for which you are clearly not gifted.

A friend of mine was discussing the future with a sixty-two-year-old widow. The widow said, "I was born to be somebody." She had a sense of destiny, not despair. You were born to be somebody. God has that special purpose for your life.

Should everyone be a professional? At times it seems that there is pressure on every teenager to go to college and become a professional person—a doctor, engineer, teacher, or social worker. But on the basis of gifts and abilities, not everyone should do this. In fact, not everyone who *can* do it necessarily *should*. Many people are unhappy in an office or a high-pressure professional environment. There are many in high-paying professions only because they were trained for it and are well-paid. They would really like to farm, work in construction, or other fields in which a college education is unnecessary. For a Christian, a job means evaluating not only what he *can* do, but what he *likes* to do and ultimately what God *calls* him to do.

A good friend of mine was highly trained in a complex scientific field. He was successful and competent. Yet he frequently expressed a desire to do something he both enjoyed and excelled in—carpentry.

Don't let the world press you into doing what does not fit your gifts *and* your emotional bent.

NOTES: 1. For further reference, see Ralph Mattson and Art Miller, *Finding a Job You Can Love* (Nashville: Thomas Nelson Publishers, 1982).

Chapter Six

WITNESS AND WORK

A VIEW OF MINISTRY

"Look out for George. If he catches you alone he'll beat you over the head with a Bible. He thinks we're all going to hell."

"Can you believe it? Darlene says she's a Christian. But look how she hurts people when they make mistakes. She never admits anything is her fault."

"I thought Jack was religious. I'd call him a hypocrite! You should see him when we travel on business."

"He's the most useless worker around. He comes late, calls in sick when I know he isn't, and now he's griping because he didn't get a raise. He better never try to dump that religious stuff on me."

Some well-meaning Christians can draw those kinds of comments all too often. Coworkers see us as we really are. We are carefully watched in all we do. We can't fool them. Witnessing to them is far different than going door-to-door or calling on church visitors—only some of whom actually know us.

Your life is a witness—for or against Christ. Your respect for people, conversations, ethics, and work habits all paint pictures of the real you. Religious talk will not dispel people's view of you if it conflicts with your actions. Those actions will inevitably be a direct result of your personal spiritual walk with Christ. If it is anemic and shallow, it will permeate your actions with inconsistency and the world's value system.

Witnessing at work is hard. There is no cookbook method, for there is no "standard" work environment. Offices, shops, small businesses, large corporations, construction, service businesses, and factories all present different contexts and different types of people. Yet some principles can help in all cases.

What is the goal of witness? It is *not* to share the gospel. It is *not* to get a convert. It is *not* to salve our consciences or fulfill some obligation to God. *It is to help people clearly understand the message of the gospel, so they can make a decision based on truth.* Therefore, our efforts must focus on helping them understand clearly, which gives room for many methods since each person comes with a particular need and background.

Before we share some principles and ideas, we want to assure you that we are not gifted evangelists. We do not have the gift of an evangelist. We have often been fearful and have often made mistakes and offended people. Yet through the years, we have seen our friends and relatives come to Christ. Not all, but some. We are still learning.

Recall from Chapter 1 that we are to be *salt* and *light* in our society. We cannot be that kind of influence unless we are involved in every segment of society. The only places this can happen are in

▶ our job,
▶ our neighborhood,
▶ our extended family.

Have you ever wondered why you are a construction worker and not a doctor? Or a factory worker and not a factory manager? Or a teacher and not a bus driver? God has sovereignly placed you where you are with your particular ability, background, and circumstances. Because of the level of income in your job, you naturally buy or rent in certain neighborhoods. Whether we like it or not, neighborhoods segregate according to social and financial levels. Instead of envying those who have more than you have, thank God for placing you in both your job, your neighborhood, and your extended family, so you can be salt and light for Christ where you are.

Of these three, the job is the only place close association is actually *forced* upon you. Thus, maximize your witness there. Because society is becoming more and more private, neighbors don't know each other as they once did. People isolate themselves in their backyards behind high fences. Many people purposely avoid knowing their neighbors. And the problem is compounded in that the average American moves every four or five years.

But don't give up in your neighborhood. Be a part of any activity there. Attend the PTA. Help in community social efforts. Invite your neighbors into your home. Help them when there is an illness or apparent need. When your children play with neighbors, use that as an opportunity to meet the parents. It can be done—if *you* make the effort. Women are often the most effective in making neighborhood contacts.

How do you actually witness on the job or in the neighborhood?

The most obvious way is by your *actions*. People see how you work and react to difficult situations. They see if you cheat your employer on the "little" things, if you get angry, or if you always protect your own interests. The way you work and act provides the framework for the opportunities to share verbally what you believe.

The second kind of witness is your *character*—the real person deep down inside. People do judge the kind of person you are. They tend to judge your motives to the extent that they perceive them.

"Bob doesn't say much, but he's got a heart of gold. He'd give you the shirt off his back."

"Bill talks a good line, but there's something phony about him—he's trying to get the boss's job."

"Have you noticed that he works when the boss is around, but how lazy he is the rest of the time?"

Others are attracted or repelled by the kind of person they believe you are.

Two brothers became Christians in a small community. They were both involved in well-known firms. Both became very verbal about their new relationship in Christ, yet people believed the one and ridiculed the other. Why? Because in one brother they saw a distinct change in character and business methods. In the other they only heard talk. God must change us on the inside or our witness will be ignored.

The third witness is what you *say*. Through words you communicate your faith in Christ. Do you know how to share your faith? Can you share your personal testimony? Can you turn a conversation from ordinary matters to spiritual things? Are you timid or unsure about telling others of Christ? We strongly recommend two books that clearly teach effective methods of witnessing: *How to Give Away Your Faith* by Paul Little (InterVarsity Press, 1966) and *Evangelism for Our Generation* by Jim Petersen (NavPress, 1985).

CONCEPTS OF WITNESS

Here are a number of specific suggestions for having an effective witness where you work. Some may not apply to you, due to your personal work circumstances. Undoubtedly there are exceptions to many of them. We do not presume they are complete or absolute. But we do believe that if these suggestions are followed you will see your witness at work improve greatly or even reverse, if you have hindered your witness in the past.

The social environment. We believe you must be part of the social environment of the people with whom you work. Except in unusual cases, you will not relate to and reach them in the work environment alone. Go to office parties. Be part of the sports teams—softball, bowling, etc. Go to the picnics, going-away parties, and banquets. Whenever possible, accept invitations to people's homes, children's graduations, children's sports events, or any event where you will meet your coworkers' spouses and families.

Open your own home for these events. You may say that you don't like many of these parties due to excessive drinking or other factors. Nor do we. But we committed to be there. In all of our years of secular military or business social events, with one exception, we were never pressured to compromise any of our personal convictions. The point is not to enjoy the events, but to be *with* friends.

If you are serious about your witness, make these events a high priority, above most Christian activities. Recently our Sunday school class had a Christmas party at our home. Even though we were their hosts (and the teacher), we urged class members not to come if they could be at any event with nonChristians.

Know your coworkers. Get to know your friends at work on a personal basis. Make note of personal items and remember them—spouse's name, children's names and ages, parents' and children's special interests (sports, hobbies, etc.), background (education, hometown, etc.), special concerns, and religious background. This will help you understand them and get into their lives. Develop genuine friendships.[1]

Listen. Listen to them. Take them seriously. Ask questions, but don't pry. Look for opportunities to hear them. Incidentally, you will find that few nonbelievers will reciprocate. Seldom will they ask you questions or be a good listener to you. Being interested in others is not a natural value for most. Also, if they know you are "religious" they will often be even less inquisitive.

Meet needs. Look for needs to meet. Be alert to such situations as illness in the family, death of a parent, death or intense problems of spouse or children (drugs, divorce, rebellion), workload or conflict with supervisors. Offer help. Take a meal to the home. Offer to baby-sit. Show care and concern. Suggest references of specialists who could help. Don't pass up an opportunity to involve yourself in their personal lives.

Won't this take time and energy? Yes. But if we are too busy in Christian activities or our own family activities to see and meet the needs of nonChristians, we are too busy. These are door openers to sharing the gospel. But we must help with no strings attached—and certainly no religious tract taped to the meal we provide.

Always be sensitive to their response. It may be that others have already met needs, and our presence would be a burden. In that case, small indicators of our concern would be in order. An encouraging note, a phone call with a specific offer of help, or a willingness to listen during lunch break at work.

Pray regularly for your coworkers by name and by need.

Know them. Know where your friends come from in terms of religious background. We suggest thinking of them in three categories—religious, but not understanding the gospel; religious, but now totally secular in outlook (a liberal church background, but no present interest); no religious background or interest at all. Each of these outlooks requires a different communication. For instance, sharing the gospel directly with one who has no religious background comes across as gibberish, a foreign language. They simply have no context in which it relates. We unknowingly develop a Christian jargon that has great meaning to us, but little or no meaning to nonChristians. Words like salvation, believe, faith, repent, know Christ, and sacrifice simply confuse the nonbeliever hearing the gospel for the first time—and also those who have heard it often. Avoid these Christian "code-words."

Introduce them to the Bible. In these days of increasing secularism, people need to study the Bible for themselves more than they need us to present the gospel. They need to discover the gospel. After they express an interest in Jesus, try to help them discover the truth from the Bible. One of the best ways is to involve them in a small Bible study where few, if any, other Christians attend. I highly recommend Bob and Betty Jacks' book, *Your Home a Lighthouse* (NavPress, 1987) to help you know how to do this. Our goal has been to help people really understand the gospel rather than just hear a recitation of the gospel—but never understand it.

Know how to share your personal testimony and the gospel. Write out your personal testimony. How did you meet Christ? What convinced you to believe in Him? Learn to share the facts of the gospel using a method such as The Navigators' Bridge Illustration or Campus Crusade's *Four Spiritual Laws.* But don't think that this will be the totality of your witness. It is but one part shared at a strategic time to aid their personal understanding.

Be competent in your job. Incompetence, laziness, or poor work will never help your witness. Competence simply eliminates a barrier and may open some doors. Much of this book relates to competence on the job.

Keep in touch. Witness is rarely short-term. Keep in touch with people through the years. Even when they leave your department or company or city, try to keep contact. You may have opportunities in years to come to help them. For us, as people who are not gifted evangelists, the long-term contacts of five to twenty years have been the most fruitful.

These are positive things to do. Are there dangers to avoid? Yes. Some of the following suggestions are controversial since they are often-used methods. If you are fruitful using them, do not let us dissuade you. We heard of one man who bluntly asked almost everyone he met, "If you were to die today, where would you go—heaven or hell?" Surprisingly, his personality allowed him to use this approach. But to most nonChristians, it would only be an irritant. Consider these "don'ts."

Don't take work time to witness. You are paid to do a job. Except in unusual cases (a business owner or a top manager whose time is at his discretion) witnessing on the job will only cause trouble over the long term. It cheats your employer. If you get into a discussion, simply say, "Let's get together and talk about this over lunch tomorrow," or arrange to talk elsewhere.

Don't use tracts. We are not opposed to all use of tracts, but they are not best at work where we see people daily. If you use them at all, make sure they are tactful and well done.

Don't give "junk" books. If you give people books to read, give good ones—well written, good paper and quality production. We once gave a relative a book for Christmas. Later, after receiving Christ, she admitted she burned everything we ever gave her except that book. It was hardbound, and she couldn't bring herself to burn an expensive book. It was a good lesson. If you give books, give good ones.

Don't argue. Argument seldom convinces anyone. You need not be totally passive, but don't engage in a battle of logic and debate. The Holy Spirit does the convincing, not you. In particular, we never argue the merits of creation against evolution, the flood, hypocrites, television preachers, the heathen, or the "good God" issues. Winning an argument will not convince them. You can point them to the Bible to discover for themselves. A good question to pose is, "If this issue could be resolved satisfactorily, would it significantly change your view of Christianity?" If the answer is affirmative, then you might consider studying it with them.

At this point you may reflect that you have violated most of these points. What can you do? Two things. First, resolve to change your patterns from now on. Second, if you believe you have really offended and alienated someone, go to him, apologize, and begin to rebuild your relationship with him.

PERSONAL EVALUATION

We witness of "what we have seen and heard" (1 John 1:3), not of the theory of the Christian life. Consequently our lives need to match our talk. Take some time here to do some personal evaluation.

At the risk of oversimplification, think of all of your life as centering on the four areas shown below: your relationship with Christ, your family, your job, and your ministry.

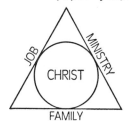

Having a right relationship with Jesus Christ is the first and most important dimension of a truly fulfilled Christian life. "Since, then, you have been raised with Christ, set your hearts on things above, where Christ is seated at the right hand of God. Set your minds on things above, not on earthly things" (Colossians 3:1-2).

This means believing in Christ as your personal Savior. It means you are committed to a daily, in-depth walk with Christ, which clearly governs the course of your life—you aren't simply going through the motions of Christian activity.

This is where many fail to lay a proper foundation. if you haven't lived a truly committed Christian life before, you certainly cannot bear a credible witness at work.

The family is the second most important dimension in a fulfilled life. "Wives, submit to your husbands. . . . Husbands, love your wives. . . . Children, obey your parents" (Colossians 3:18-21). Men find it easy to give their jobs higher priority than their family, while women may place more importance on the family than on their relationship with Christ. Both are wrong. No other human relationships are more important than family relationships.

The third dimension concerns our *job* and career, the fundamental purpose of which is providing for the needs of our family. When the focus becomes self-fulfillment, prestige, or wealth, we pervert the most basic purpose of work. But God does want us to enjoy what we do and He wants us to do it heartily—not for man's approval, but His. Our job is a platform for a public demonstration of the Christian life.

The final dimension is that of our ministry. We are to reach out to others with the love and life we enjoy in Christ. "Be wise in the way you act toward outsiders; make the most of every opportunity" (Colossians 4:5). We need an outward focus as well as a relationship with Christ, our family, and our job. We should be actively involved in helping others discover life in Christ.

Avoid neglecting any of these four areas. Without Christ, our life is without a dependable, unifying force. When any of the other three areas are shortchanged, the imbalance can result in frustration and failure.

EVALUATION

We need to translate subjective feelings into objective facts to evaluate true success in life. Look at the following statements to pinpoint areas of strength and areas of need. Determine which statements are true in your life.

Relationship with Christ

1. I have private Bible reading and prayer at least four days a week.   _____
2. I have done personal, written Bible study at least four times in the last six months.   _____
3. I have at least one friend with whom I have significant interaction on personal, spiritual issues.   _____
4. I have made one or more significant changes in my life in the past year in direct response to God's urging.   _____
5. Recent conflict with another has been resolved and is not bothering me now.   _____
6. So far as I know, I am not resisting God on any major issue.   _____
7. I have clearly received Christ as my personal Savior.   _____
8. I am satisfactorily established in a local church fellowship.   _____

Family

1. In the last month I have done some activity alone with each of my children. _____
2. In the last month I have had some quality private time outside the home to spend with my spouse. _____
3. In the last month I have had no more than one significant conflict with my spouse. _____
4. We have had family devotions at least once in the last week. _____
5. I have prayed privately with my spouse in the last month. _____
6. I have not even considered divorce in the past year. _____
7. I have a good relationship with each of my children. _____
8. My job allows me enough personal time with my family. _____

Job

1. I have a job. _____
2. My basic material needs are being met. _____
3. I have been able to provide adequately for myself and the family. _____
4. I have never been fired. _____
5. I am basically successful in my work. _____
6. I have been promoted fairly and regularly according to merit. _____
7. I look forward to going to work most of the time. _____
8. I am free from any major conflicts with others at work. _____

Ministry

1. I now have a specific, personal ministry.   ____
2. I can identify a specific spiritual gift or ability that God has given me.   ____
3. I am using this gift or ability now.   ____
4. I have between one and three major church responsibilities.   ____
5. I have led someone outside my family to salvation in Christ.   ____
6. I believe I am making a vital contribution to someone's life outside my family.   ____
7. I believe that God is using me now.   ____

Now look back over the lists. If you remember feeling a pang of depression or fear in answering any statement, put a check by it and plan to evaluate this area of your life more closely. In our use of this test we have found that a positive response to fifty percent of the statements is too low. A score between sixty and seventy percent still shows a significant need.

CONCEPT OF A PERSONAL MINISTRY

Ministry. Isn't that what ministers do? Isn't it just the paid clergy who have a ministry? Absolutely not.

Ministry is a word that describes something every Christian should do. The word *minister* comes from a Latin word meaning "servant." A ministry is serving others with the gifts and abilities God gave you.

Should a ministry be a full-time occupation?

No. A full-time ministry should be the exception rather than the rule.

Most ministry is done by the laity—men and women

who live and work in the world. Ideally, a full-time pastor or worker is a specialist and a facilitator who helps the laity do *their* ministry.

So what exactly is a ministry? A ministry is a specific task to which you are called by God—either in the Body of Christ or in reaching the lost. It could be teaching Sunday school, evangelism, serving, or any number of other functions of the Body.

You can have a ministry only when your relationship to Christ, family, and job are balanced. Your ministry should flow out of your life. First, as shared before, your life must be centered in Christ; you must be growing as His disciple and submitted to His lordship.[2] Second, if your family life is not in order, you have no stable home base from which to minister. Third, you need to maintain a witness in your job by how you work.

DEFINITION OF MINISTRY

Now let's be specific on types and definitions of ministry. There are two basic types of ministry:

> ▶ Outreach ministry. This is reaching out to nonChristians to help them come to know Christ. It can include direct witnessing as well as serving and helping others.
> ▶ Ministry to the Body of Christ. This is a ministry to those who are already Christians. This type of ministry breaks down into two categories:
> > *Discipling*, which includes following up on new Christians and helping them grow to maturity;
> > *Caring for* (or shepherding) those in the Body who have special needs (the elderly, the sick, and those who need counseling, for example).

Every Christian should do some ministry of both types—evangelism and ministry to the Body. But how? What practical things can we do in these two areas?

OUTREACH

The foundation for outreach to the lost is a firm conviction that we have a direct commission from God to reach the world for Christ. "But you will receive power when the Holy Spirit comes on you; and *you will be my witnesses* in Jerusalem, and in all Judea and Samaria, and to the ends of the earth" (Acts 1:8). We have no option. We must witness to those who don't know Christ. But we need to learn how. Witnessing involves more than giving out tracts or bringing people to a gospel meeting at church. We need to know other ways to reach out. Here are some suggestions:

Conduct an investigative Bible study. This is a study in your home with nonChristians who have agreed to study a portion of the Bible for four to six weeks. We've used the Gospel of John.[3]

Conduct a women's evangelistic tea or coffee. Simply invite primarily nonChristian women to your home for tea or coffee and to hear a brief presentation by another woman. This would usually be a testimony or stimulating discussion of an interesting topic related to the gospel. Later you could organize a home Bible study or meet with some of the women individually to share the gospel in more detail.[4]

Have people in your home. Use your home as a point of outreach. Invite people in for dinner, to watch a football game on television, for dessert, or for games. Befriend them and let them see what a Christian home is like. Look for natural opportunities for sharing your faith.

Neighborhood evangelism. Begin praying for your neighbors. Invite them in socially at various times. Organize a neighborhood Bible study with women, men, or couples.

Problem counseling with nonChristians. Keep alert for those at work or in your neighborhood who are hurting and in need. Marriage problems, difficulties with teens, or physical illness can all provide opportunities to serve and help. Through helping them you may have the opportunity to share Christ as you demonstrate His love.

Calling on church contacts. Visitors to your church are natural contacts for evangelism. Programs like Evangelism Explosion use a church visitation program to secure opportunities for presenting the gospel.

Children's evangelism. Children are fertile ground for the gospel. Most people make their commitment for Christ when they are children or teens. Child Evangelism Fellowship and similar organizations are good vehicles for reaching children in the community. Through children you may also reach their parents.

Youth outreach. Some people relate well to teens and should put their efforts into an outreach to them. Church youth groups, and organizations like Youth for Christ and Young Life, have opportunities for adults to serve by helping to reach teenagers.

All of these are fine ideas, but ideas do not work by themselves. The key is to *do something*, not just talk or think about it. Often we are reluctant to evangelize because we do not know how to share the plan of salvation. Learn how to do this from your pastor, or friends, so you can clearly share the gospel.

MINISTRY TO BELIEVERS

A ministry to the Body of Christ is also necessary. Not everyone can preach or be a great leader. But there are many vital opportunities and essential services that most people can fill behind the scenes. Here are some suggestions:

Teaching. Sunday schools are usually short of good teachers for adults, young people, and children. If you do teach, become involved in the lives of your students. Give your time to the children in social events, outings, and personal contact. They need interaction with adults to help them come to know Christ and to grow and mature.

Club programs. Christian Service Brigade, Awana, and Pioneer Ministries, as well as other church youth programs, provide opportunities for adults to develop in-depth relationships with children other than on Sunday mornings. Dedicated leaders are greatly needed to work with young people and children in the context of crafts, outdoor events, and practical skills. Children respond to down-to-earth contacts. Many nonChristian children who attend these programs can be reached for Christ.

Church offices. The task of an elder or deacon is one of the most important in the church. Elders do not simply meet for church business. Rather they provide a significant ministry to people.

Music. Many people enjoy music and can participate in the choir or other music programs. Children's choirs provide a valuable service by helping children learn to love music and to worship through music.

Home Bible studies for Christians. One of the most rewarding contexts for fellowship in the church is a small group studying the Word on a regular basis. You can either lead, be a participant, or simply open your home. This is one of the few places where you get involved in personal investigation of Scripture. Also, you develop deep relationships with others in the study.

Planning. Every church needs people who can plan the activities and direction of the fellowship. The pastor cannot do it all. Committees and short-term planning teams will always need people who are eager to serve and help. Much of this effort involves behind-the-scenes hard work that someone must do. These people are special load-lifters for the pastor and the entire congregation. The idea for an event is just the beginning. The detailed execution requires ninety percent of the work.

Hospitality. Some people minister through hospitality. They open their homes, invite people in, and make them feel welcome. This is far more than simple entertainment. It involves extending yourself when it may not be convenient, as well as when you plan for it. Hospitality is a special gift. It includes bringing others, both Christians and nonChristians, into your home and family and extending yourself beyond your normal social obligations.

Person-to-person discipling. Learn to help another person grow to maturity in Christ. Seldom does one grow to his full capacity as a natural byproduct of simply attending church. Much spiritual learning is communicated on a person-to-person basis. In this intimate way people open their lives and share real needs.[5]

Person-to-person counseling. Counseling presents one of the most demanding burdens in a pastor's work. Usually, by the time he is consulted, a problem is quite serious. Many people can learn to counsel effectively in problem situations. If you find yourself frequently listening to others' problems, you may be one with whom people share easily. This gives you the opportunity to help *if* you are qualified through experience or training and know what to do. Think of the load this would lift for the pastoral staff of your church. A key is getting some training as well as knowing the limits of your counseling ability.

Youth ministry. Every church needs people who can work effectively with the youth. It is a task with special demands. You must relate to them on a personal basis, open your home to them, and be available at odd hours. Teenagers need both couples and singles who will be their adult confidants and counselors.

Serving. Many tasks in the Body involve simply serving—doing things behind the scenes to make activities easier for others. Mailings, secretarial work, finances, janitorial work, printing, and building repairs must be done. But they do not get done without someone taking responsibility. If you are gifted in one of these areas, you can make a significant personal contribution by serving.

Administration. This is closely related to serving. Administrators can handle business items and help a church function properly. Building scheduling, transportation, and budgeting are only a few of the tasks in this type of ministry.

Missions. A church without a missions program is like a body without a soul—empty and focused only on itself. But a concern for missions does not just materialize. It takes concerned people who plan how to make others more aware of world needs and who can motivate people to pray and give. Each church should keep in touch with the missionaries it supports, know their needs and current concerns. Churches don't write letters, people do. You could have a ministry by writing to your church's missionaries.

Knowing what can be done as a ministry is still a far cry from doing it. Knowledge is ten percent. Action is ninety percent. Even though one is mentally convinced that a personal ministry is essential for a growing Christian, identifying a sphere of service and starting is often difficult. First, consider what every Christian should do.

THE STANDARD FOR ALL CHRISTIANS

No one can do everything, but everyone can do something. Certain fundamental activities must be part of every Christian's life if he or she is to be happy, balanced, and fulfilled in his or her personal ministry.

▶Every Christian should do some kind of evangelism or outreach. When we minister only to those in the Body of Christ we turn inward and lose our vision for the lost.

▶Every Christian should develop one major ministry involvement of either the outreach or Body ministry type. This one ministry is what you concentrate upon and give yourself to. All others become subservient to it. Too many people try to do too many things and so do none of them well. Concentrate solidly on one strategic activity.

▶Every Christian should be discipled or helped by another more mature Christian. We all need accountability and training. Seldom does one develop in a healthy way totally alone. We need a mentor, not to control us, but to train us and build us up in the faith.

▶Every Christian should be discipling another. The essence of life is physical and spiritual reproduction. We must not only aid in the birth of new Christians, but we must also help them grow and mature. This need not mean that your major ministry is discipling, but it is a part of your ministry. A parent's first responsibility is discipling his own children. Our churches are filled with people who desperately need help with their spiritual growth. But few Christians are willing to help or know how to help.

The underlying prerequisites for any ministry are our personal walk with God and a deep love for others. Without these elements you will not have a ministry—only activities and schedules. Without a deep walk with God, your ministry may appear religious but will actually be hollow and empty. Don't neglect your own spiritual life.

HOW TO SELECT YOUR MINISTRY

Make a copy of the chart below. First, review the kinds of ministry listed in this chapter. Add other ministries as you think of them. Mark those you are currently involved in with a check in the first column. Next, put a check in the second column for those ministries you have done in the past.

Review the list again, and put a check in the third column by those ministries you feel you could do with proper training. Include those that you have already done or are already doing. Finally, select three or four activities from each section that you would like to try if you had the opportunity. Put a check by these activities in the fourth column. You can include ones you are already doing, if you still want to keep doing them.

MINISTRY INTEREST AND ABILITY SURVEY

	Already Doing	Have Done Before	Could Do	Would Like to Try
Outreach				
Ministry to believers				

You have now completed a rough interest and ability survey for your potential ministry. You can use this chart in several ways. It will form the basis of a later activity—actually selecting your ministry. See how many checks in the last column match up with checks in the first column. The more they match, the better. The fewer matches or correlations, the more likely you will want to alter your activity schedule.

Now to actually plan your ministry. Refer to the questionnaire on page 107. Before you can plan, you need to evaluate where you stand now. These questions will help you identify your personal needs.

The chart on page 108 will help you plan for your ministry. The personal growth section helps you discover if you need to prepare before launching into your ministry. From the chart on page 105, select two or three items under "Would-Like-to-Try." Then make a specific plan for each of them. You need not do them all at once, but can stagger them over several weeks.

As you evaluate yourself and try to determine your best ministry, discuss it with your spouse, family, pastor, and a close Christian friend. They can give you good insight into yourself. Then try one of the ministries on a small scale for a few weeks or months. For instance, you might substitute as a teacher or observe a class for a while. After you have tried it, evaluate your performance. Then you could try another ministry for a short time.

Determine what further training or instruction you need in order to do a particular ministry. If you need to develop some special skills such as counseling, leadership, or leading Bible studies, don't delay learning those skills. Finally, plan on entering your ministry completely within one year. The chart on page 109 may help you set some specific goals.

PLANNING MY MINISTRY: CURRENT SITUATION

1. What ministry activities am I currently involved in?

_____

_____

_____

_____

2. Considering the four "musts" for a Christian,

   What evangelism am I doing? _____

   _____

   What is my *major* ministry? _____

   Who is helping me grow? _____

   Who am I discipling? _____

3. Of the ministries listed in item 1, which coincide with the "Would-Like-to-Try" column of the ministry survey?

   _____

   _____

4. Do I believe that I am now doing my *major* ministry?

   Yes _____   No _____

5. If not, do I have time to add another ministry activity without canceling something else?

   Yes _____   No _____

6. If I cannot add another ministry activity, what current activity could I delete? _____

   _____

PLANNING MY MINISTRY: FOR THE FUTURE

PERSONAL GROWTH	Satisfactory	Need to Do What I Know	Need Further Help
Daily devotions			
Personal Bible study			
Prayer			
Witnessing			

MINISTRY	Can Do It Now	Must Get Training	Training Available
1.			
2.			
3.			
4.			
5.			

SPECIFIC PLAN FOR MY MINISTRY

Specific plan for _____
                          (name the ministry)

                                    Date to accomplish

1. Investigate opportunities.   _____

2. Find out how to get training.   _____

3. Get training.   _____

4. Begin this ministry.   _____

Specific plan for _____
                          (name the ministry)

                                    Date to accomplish

1. Investigate opportunities.   _____

2. Find out how to get training.   _____

3. Get training.   _____

4. Begin this ministry.   _____

Specific plan for _____
                          (name the ministry)

                                    Date to accomplish

1. Investigate opportunities.   _____

2. Find out how to get training.   _____

3. Get training.   _____

4. Begin this ministry.   _____

NOTES: 1. See "Friendship with NonChristians," in *Friends and Friendship*, by Jerry and Mary White (Colorado Springs, Colo.: NavPress, 1982).
2. See Walter A. Henrichsen, *Disciples Are Made—Not Born* (Wheaton, Ill.: Victor Books/Scripture Press, 1974).
3. As we mentioned earlier, you may want to consider *Your Home a Lighthouse*, by Bob and Betty Jacks (Colorado Springs, Colo.: NavPress, 1987).
4. A helpful aid for organizing and leading a women's evangelistic Bible study is *Jesus Cares for Women*, by Helene Ashker (Colorado Springs, Colo.: NavPress, 1988).
5. To help another Christian grow, read LeRoy Eims' book *The Lost Art of Disciplemaking* (Colorado Springs, Colo.: NavPress, 1978). Also refer to Francis Cosgrove's book *Essentials of Discipleship* (Colorado Springs, Colo.: NavPress, 1980).

Chapter Seven

GETTING AHEAD— NO MATTER WHAT

It was Gary's first day on the job. His reputation as a brilliant scientist and an up-and-coming manager had preceded him. He was friendly to everyone and rapidly made the rounds to get to know his departmental personnel. But after several weeks it became clear that he found the right people to talk to and work with. He developed friendships with those who could serve him or aid his reputation. His ego and ambitions came first. And he was successful. He was soon assigned to choice projects where he even recruited some of his old "friends" to work for him. But instead of finding the friendly Gary they once knew, they now found a man with power and influence who was simply using them for his own advancement.

THE DILEMMA OF AMBITION

We can easily picture the classic ambitious man in our minds. He gets ahead by any means. He claws his way to the top. He disregards those who get hurt in his reach for success. He is pleasant when it serves his purpose and indifferent when he is not served. Though much of what he does helps the organization, we sense that his motive is totally self-serving. His goal may be position, money, or power.

Not only is this man trying to be president of the company, but he is also the factory worker trying to be foreman. He is the Christian trying to run the committee. She is the wife pushing her husband and striving for status. He is the clerk moonlighting at another job to make more money. He is the father directing his children's lives, trying to achieve success vicariously through them.

Does that sound wrong? Of course it does. It *is* wrong. But if ambition is wrong, should we seek to remove all ambition? Let's look at ambition's opposite.

Joe Ambitionless. We know him, too. His house and yard are a mess. He watches TV for hours every night. He never initiates family activities. His children run wild without discipline or direction. He is a Christian pew-sitter—doctrinally straight but totally uninvolved. He never accepts a responsibility by choice. In his job he is concerned only about security and adequate money. Is this the Christian standard? Of course not!

That is the dilemma. Too much ambition leads to presumptuous self-promotion. Too little ambition displays laziness and slothfulness. How much is too much? How much is too little?

Ambition itself is neither bad nor good. It is a part of our nature, like hunger, desire, or love. But hunger can become gluttony; desire can become craving; love can become lust. And ambition can become selfishness and pride. Like any normal drive, it can be misdirected.

Even the world recognizes the limits of ambition.

Managers or executives who aren't ambitious aren't worth their salt—they probably shouldn't be leaders in the first place. But people who are overly ambitious, or ambitious in the wrong way, not only hurt their own chances, they may ruin their health as well.

When we are so dominated by personal ambition that we fail to recognize the equally justified ambitions of others, we lose our perspective. If our ambition is greater than our ability, we will also be victims of constant tension and frustration.

But a human desire to succeed is one thing; preoccupation with personal ambition that keeps us constantly wound up, frustrated and fretting about our future prospects, is another. Carried to an extreme, it's a big stumbling block to our continued progress, not to mention our peace of mind.[1]

The Bible does not condemn ambition, but it does condemn wrong *motives* prompting ambition, such as selfishness, pride, or greed. It does not condemn lack of ambition, but it may condemn the lack of faith and obedience. If the Scriptures lean in either direction, it is to encourage us to have godly ambition. "Make it your ambition to lead a quiet life" (1 Thessalonians 4:11). Paul's ambition was to "press on toward the goal for the prize of the upward call of God in Christ Jesus" (Philippians 3:14) and to "know Him, and the power of His resurrection" (Philippians 3:10). The Lord Jesus Christ preached the ambition to serve when He said, "If anyone wants to be first, he shall be last of all, and servant of all" (Mark 9:35).

We must be more specific to understand this in the biblical context. A dictionary definition of *ambition* is "(1) strong desire to gain a particular objective, specifically the drive to succeed, or to gain fame, power, wealth, etc.; (2) the objectives strongly desired." Therefore the right use of ambition depends on the following:

▶ the rightness of the goal,
▶ the rightness of the motive for reaching that goal.

"Whatever you do, do your work heartily, as for the Lord rather than for men; knowing that from the Lord you will receive the reward of the inheritance. It is the Lord Christ whom you serve" (Colossians 3:23-24). This passage is packed with meaning for the working person. The only legitimate goal is to serve Christ. If serving Christ is our motive, the matter of promotion or raises can be left in God's hand. When a person works enthusiastically, he will usually produce more than the rest of the workers. In fact, working heartily may be interpreted as a striving for advancement by coworkers. Everyone agrees with the ideal of serving Christ, but in practice it can be difficult to discern when our motive is actually right.

EVIDENCE OF UNHEALTHY AMBITION

Ambition can be misused. The problem is how to identify when ambition becomes sin. Here are a few indicators of unhealthy ambition:

Serving Your Own Ego

"But you, are you seeking great things for yourself? Do not seek them" (Jeremiah 45:5). God has no place for the Christian on an ego trip. Such a person desires to be recognized, honored, and deferred to. He is self-serving and self-centered. He often thinks, "I wonder if they saw me do that?" or "Does he know *who* I am?" or "If I were in that position, they would listen to me!" Ambition focused on personal ego will not have God's blessing. One person observed that an egotist is not a man who thinks too highly of himself, but one who thinks too little of others. It could also be expressed in how a person enters a room. One gives the impression, "Here I am!" Another enters the room and says, "Ah! There you are!"

Grasping for Position and Power

"But Jesus called them to Himself, and said, 'You know that the rulers of the Gentiles lord it over them, and their great men exercise authority over them. It is not so among you'" (Matthew 20:25-26). The *King James Version* reads, "But it shall not be so among you." The world clutches for power and authority, exercising these for personal benefit. Jesus condemns this motive. The Christian's driving force cannot be a desire for position and power. If God gives it, fine, but that is not to be the *end* goal. Guard against the desire for authority. Even in churches, misplaced ambition and grasping for leadership lead to conflicts and separations. "But it shall *not* be so among you." A grasping for position and power holds in it the seeds of death.

A Desire to Control Others

"The rulers of the Gentiles *lord* it over them, and . . . *exercise* authority . . ." (Matthew 20:25). The world's pattern is to control people for personal goals. And Christians, too, experience an inner urge to direct others, to change their thinking, and to manipulate them. The tendency is to control instead of influence. As this desire creeps forward, know that it has crossed the line from godly to unhealthy ambition.

Henry Ford once said, "The question 'who ought to be the boss?' is like the question, 'who ought to sing tenor in the quartet?' Obviously, the one who can sing tenor."

A Motive to Be Rich

"Do not weary yourself to gain wealth, cease from your consideration of it. When you set your eyes on it, it is gone.

For wealth certainly makes itself wings, like an eagle that flies toward the heavens" (Proverbs 23:4-5). Or, "Labour not to be rich" (KJV). "He who loves money will not be satisfied with money, nor he who loves abundance with its income. This too is vanity" (Ecclesiastes 5:10). The Bible discusses riches and possessions at great length. The Bible clearly teaches that money is not evil, but that "the *love* of money is a root of all sorts of evil, and some by longing for it have wandered away from the faith, and pierced themselves with many a pang" (1 Timothy 6:10).

A friend of mine stated that his goal is to be independently wealthy. This intention consumed him for years. He became discontent, had family difficulties, and never achieved independent wealth. He finally realized that he really needed to return to a deep relationship with God. Ambition for riches will not be blessed by God. It is not a legitimate goal for a Christian.

But let us discuss this a little further. In our culture with its prevailing focus on money and possessions, how can a Christian discern what is healthy? Wealth per se is not sinful. Hard work for more money is not sinful. The key is *why* we want more money. Proper reasons such as food for the family, education for our children, giving to the poor, providing employment in a business, and giving to the Lord are completely honorable.

God has provided wealth to some Christians. They give generously to the Lord's work. But the Christian who is working hard and becoming wealthy may be regarded with envy or suspicion. God gives some the gifts and abilities to be successful investors and businessmen. This is a legitimate endeavor. The only requirement is that he be a giving, spiritual Christian—that his business practices are honest, that he is generous to the Lord and others, and that the motive of his heart is *not* simply to be wealthy. A good study of this matter is Christ's parables of the talents (Matthew 25:14-30, Luke 19:12-26).

This issue is confused by the "health and wealth" emphasis of some Bible teachers. The implication is that if a believer does certain things, and makes certain promises, then God is obligated to provide health and wealth. I browsed in a bookstore in Manila, Philippines, and in the religious section found the majority of books propagating this view. Not only is it deceptive to the poor, it is unscriptural. God gives only the promise to provide for our needs, not to make us rich. He promises to care for us in time of need, not always to make us healthy or wealthy. Guard against a lust for wealth.

Personal Competition

"Do nothing from selfishness or empty conceit" (Philippians 2:3). In the Phillips version this verse reads, "Never act from motives of rivalry or personal vanity." Again, "Where jealousy and selfish ambition exist, there is disorder and every evil thing" (James 3:16). Most Americans thrive on competition. In some philosophies, winning is what counts most.

I enjoy handball much more than jogging for my physical exercise, because handball is competitive. Competition produces extra adrenalin in the system and stimulates greater activity. Competition has many benefits, but also dangers; problems arise when simple competition becomes personal rivalry. When the goal changes from doing an excellent job to "beating out" another person, competition has become an unhealthy ambition. We should compete against a standard, not another person.

The world's emphasis on competition is aptly described by Adam Smith: "You could take away all the trophies and substitute plastic heads or whales' teeth. As long as there is a way to keep score they will play."[2] Misdirected competition among Christians is especially distasteful and destructive. "But if you bite and devour one another, take care lest you be consumed by one another" (Galatians 5:15). In your job, do your work well, but guard against personal competition as a motivating force.

Richard Halverson, Chaplain of the United States Senate, graphically describes the world's standards in contrast to God's values, based on the Sermon on the Mount:

> The way of the kingdom of God is *antithetical* to the way of our contemporary culture.
>
> Our culture says, "Blessed are those who've got it together—*who've made it* . . . blessed are the achievers." Jesus said, "Blessed are the poor in spirit . . ."
>
> Our culture says, "Blessed are those who *couldn't care less*—who are on top . . . who promote self." Jesus said, "Blessed are those who mourn . . ."
>
> Our culture says, "Blessed are *the mighty*—the powerful . . . flaunt it." Jesus said, "Blessed are the meek . . ."
>
> Our culture says, "Blessed are those who are *not restrained by moral and ethical 'taboos'* . . . live it up!" Jesus said, "Blessed are those who hunger and thirst after righteousness . . ."
>
> Our culture says, "Blessed are the *manipulators*—the oppressors—the influential." Jesus said, "Blessed are the merciful . . ."
>
> Our culture says, "Blessed are the *strong*—the *drivers* . . . the *makers and doers!*" Jesus said, "Blessed are the peacemakers . . ."
>
> Our culture says, "Blessed are the *expedient*—the *compromisers* . . . the *conformists* . . . the ones who don't rock the boat!" Jesus said, "Blessed are those who are persecuted for righteousness' sake. . . ."[3]

EVIDENCE OF HEALTHY AMBITION

Healthy ambition is possible—even more, it is necessary. Each person must examine his heart motives before God, so any list of good or bad motives is inadequate. Yet, a few examples may be helpful.

The Desire to Serve God

"It is the Lord Christ whom you serve" (Colossians 3:24). The ambition to serve Christ is the highest a person can have. When you "do your work heartily" (verse 23) with this motive, God will bless your life and your work. We serve Christ primarily by being obedient to His Word. But the Bible instructs us to work diligently and honestly as a witness to those around us. Therefore we should make it our *basic* ambition to serve Christ. We are where we are because He put us there.

To Be a Witness

Our witness is determined by the quality of our work and our attitude. A lazy person will not have the respect of nonChristians; they must see the scriptural principles of diligence and honesty demonstrated.

Therefore a desire for promotion, for skill improvement, and for personal recognition can be right *if* the basic motive is to be a witness for Jesus Christ. A good test for this motive is to ask yourself, "Have I witnessed to my coworkers recently?" You must both work well *and* speak to those around you in order for them to know your motivations for good work.

Let your light shine before men in such a way that they may see your good works and glorify your Father who is in heaven. (Matthew 5:16)

Conduct yourselves with wisdom toward outsiders [nonChristians], making the most of the opportunity. (Colossians 4:5)

This should be your ambition: to live a quiet life, minding your own business and doing your own works; just as we told you before. As a result, people who are not Christians will trust and respect you. (1 Thessalonians 4:11-12, TLB)

To Influence Society
When God told Abraham of His intention to destroy Sodom and Gomorrah, He said, "If I find in Sodom fifty righteous within the city, then I will spare the whole place on their account" (Genesis 18:26). Later God said He would spare it if only ten righteous people were found (verse 32). Many times in the Old Testament, we see God using one man to influence an entire nation—not just the Abrahams, Davids, and Elijahs, but also the fearful Gideons, cowardly Jonahs, and faithful Calebs.

A Christian *can* influence society. NonChristians often experience God's blessing because of the presence and influence of Christians. To a great extent America has been blessed because of Christians in the society. The presence of one Christian can change the language in an office, restrain others from sin, influence decisions for honesty, and change the character of a neighborhood or a town.

More than once I had senior officers or bosses apologize for using foul language, when it slipped out in my presence. In the military it is a custom to throw a party upon promotion—usually a cocktail party. Six associates and I were promoted to various ranks about the same time, and three of us were Christians. We presented the idea of hosting a prime rib dinner rather than a cocktail party. It was more expensive but all liked the idea. This was a creative alternative that influenced even a longstanding tradition.

An ambition to influence society is worthy. This may be a prompting motive for entering politics or joining the PTA, secular service clubs, or other community endeavors. In many of these activities, influence is greater if you are highly respected in your job and profession.

To Be Used by God

Elisha was a farmer, called to ministry by Elijah while plowing in the fields (1 Kings 19:19-21). After some time of serving Elijah (1 Kings 19:21, 2 Kings 3:11), he asked, "Please, let a double portion of your spirit be upon me" (2 Kings 2:9). The context makes it clear that he deeply wanted to be used by God.

Solomon prayed, "Give Thy servant an understanding heart to judge Thy people to discern between good and evil" (1 Kings 3:9). When Solomon prayed to be used by God to serve others, God also blessed him with riches and honor (verse 13).

Paul specifically prayed for Christians in Colossae to be "bearing fruit in every good work and increasing in the knowledge of God; strengthened with all power" (Colossians 1:10-11). God will bless a deep desire to be used by Him. To be used in a particular place or way may require certain position, status, or education. Thus a goal that in itself could be selfish ambition can be legitimate if undergirded with the deep desire to be used by God.

In 1961, I sensed that God was leading me to teach at the Air Force Academy, where I could minister to cadets. But to do this I needed to obtain a master's degree. I had no deep ambition to return to school, but I did so to allow God to send me to the Air Force Academy. Education or status was not the goal, but obeying God was.

To Lead Spiritually

"It is a trustworthy statement; if any man aspires to the office of overseer, it is a fine work he desires to do" (1 Timothy 3:1). To seek spiritual leadership and influence is commendable. However, the list of qualifications following 1 Timothy 3:1 must be met. If they are not met, a person may be "conceited and fall into the condemnation incurred by the devil" (verse 6). A good discussion of spiritual leadership can be found in Oswald Sander's book *Spiritual Leadership* (Moody Press, 1967). Howard Butt expresses the motivation well: "If you believe in Christ, you lead to love, outside of Christ you love to lead."[4]

To Best Use Your Spiritual Gift

"And since we have gifts that differ according to the grace given to us, let each exercise them accordingly" (Romans 12:6). God has given us particular gifts and abilities, and we are responsible for developing and using them. It is worthy to aspire to be trained or to have a position to use a specific gift. Sometimes gifts will coincide with abilities needed in a secular job. Although we should discover and develop our gifts, we should beware of this one thing: we cannot discover and develop our gifts unless we are growing as disciples and are doing those things commanded for every Christian (such as studying the Word, witnessing, obeying). God is interested in our daily walk with Him first of all.

I was traveling in India while writing this chapter. In that context, much of this discussion seems ironic. The unemployment rate exceeds fifty percent in many parts of India. Indian students told me that only forty to fifty percent of those with bachelor's degrees will obtain jobs immediately after college graduation; for those with master's degrees, about sixty percent will find work; with doctorates, seventy percent. The rest may spend three or four years trying to find a job, and then many will resort to changing their career fields.

Thus I wondered if any of these thoughts on "getting ahead" applied to Indian students. As I discussed this with a Christian student, I found that the same *motives* were there. He asked me whether it was wrong to desire a car or a house. Not necessarily a *nice* car or a *fancy* house—just a car and a house. Quite a difference in perspective, isn't it? The *motives* for ambition are the same in India as they are here.

In summary, we conclude that ambition in itself is neither bad nor good, but the motives behind ambition must be examined in the light of Scripture. We must return to the three key principles.

First, God is totally in charge of our present and our future, and He will promote, prosper, or place us as He pleases. "For promotion cometh neither from the east, nor from the west, nor from the south. But God is the judge: he putteth down one, and setteth up another" (Psalm 75:6-7, KJV).

Second, each person must personally search out God's will for each decision and ambition. No one can judge our motives; we are personally and completely responsible for our decisions. "So then do not be foolish, but understand what the will of the Lord is" (Ephesians 5:17). However, we should not neglect to seek counsel from godly, mature Christians. "The way of a fool is right in his own eyes, but a wise man is he who listens to counsel" (Proverbs 12:15).

Third, our worth does not depend on whether we have great or small ability, much or little position, great or small riches. We must remember this: "For who makes you different from anybody else, and what have you got that was not given to you? And if anything has been given to you, why boast of it as if you had achieved it yourself?" (1 Corinthians 4:7, PH).

WHAT COST PROMOTION?

Howard walked out of the manager's office as if floating on air. He had just been offered a promotion to exactly the kind of job he had dreamed of for years. It would mean a raise in pay and a secure status in the company. The only catch was that he would have to move three times in two years and finally settle in a large eastern city: a small price for such a significant offer.

Then his heart sank. He thought of his eight-year-old son. John had a birth defect that required special training. The family had moved here specifically because that training was available.

Howard shared the news with his wife. She too had mixed emotions. She wanted the best both for him and for John. So they talked, prayed, and reviewed what God was doing in their lives. Howard had an excellent influence and testimony at the company; two of his coworkers had received Christ, and he was helping them to grow. Howard's two older children, Susan and Rick, had found their niche in a group of Christian teenagers at their church. In fact, Howard and his wife had come to the city five years ago as young, indifferent Christians. God had gotten their attention through John's problem, and they sought spiritual help in a local church. They found a strong, Bible-teaching ministry and a layman who helped them to grow personally.

The family reasoned that they could probably find similar circumstances in the other cities along with help for John, and Howard could perhaps be apart from the family for part of the training. But the more they prayed, the less peace they felt regarding the promotion. After three weeks of careful consideration and counseling, Howard decided to refuse the promotion even though it very likely meant no further opportunities would be offered. The cost of promotion was simply too much to pay.

A hard decision? Certainly. Foolish? No. We must allow God to lead in every circumstance. There are times when the world's system and standards simply will not give guidance to a Christian. The story of Howard is a composite of many people we have counseled over the years, but whose dilemma repeats itself daily in the lives of believers.

What are you willing to sacrifice to get ahead in your job: your family? your ministry? your personal spiritual growth? In many decisions you will sacrifice one or more of these, unless you weigh all the factors carefully.

Sameer was a Palestinian refugee living in Lebanon. He became a Christian through the witness of friends. He was discipled while in the University of Beirut, where he received a degree in business administration. In his first day on a sales job in a Kuwait chemical firm, his employer told him, "Sameer, the first thing I want you to understand is, this job is to be your god. We require this of our men."

Sameer said a quick prayer, looked his new boss in the eye, and said, "Sorry, I already have a God. But I'll make a bargain with you. I'll work for you, and if I can't sell more in giving this company my second best than anybody you've got here who has made the company his god, you can fire me." Sameer's employer was startled but agreed to the bargain.

It was not easy, but Sameer worked hard and put God first and the company second. His second was better than anyone else's first. He became responsible for contract negotiations in all Asia for this firm. God clearly honored Sameer's decision on priorities.

God will honor you if you put Him first in every aspect of your life. "Seek first His kingdom and His righteousness; and all these things shall be added to you" (Matthew 6:33). Christ clearly demands first priority. If your job causes you to neglect your spiritual life, you are walking on dangerous ground.

Many jobs do demand a great deal of time and effort. As a Christian, you have a responsibility to demonstrate loyalty to your employer. When there is extra work to be done, you should do your part. But when the job demands your life, the priority is too high.

When opportunity for promotion does occur, weigh carefully its effects on your life. We suggest that you consider these factors:

▶Your ability. Can you handle the new job without excessive time?

▶Your location. Will it require change? (Chapter 11 examines this topic in detail.)

▶Your motive. Why do you want the promotion?

▶Your family. What impact will it have on your family life and on individual family members?

▶Your spiritual life. Will you be hindered in your personal growth?

▶Your spiritual ministry. Will it increase or decrease your effectiveness for Christ?

Many men and women have sacrificed the family for their career. They work excessive hours, bring work home, undertake heavy social obligations, and focus on advancement. Meanwhile the family is neglected; the children are raised by others or by the wife alone. Yes, they have all they need materially, but no parents. As the children become teenagers, they begin to live their own lives. Drugs, rebellion, and resentment take control of them, and suddenly parents realize that they gave their lives to the wrong things. Now the career seems meaningless, but it is too late. The damage has been done.

I look back on my early years in the space business and see that I was driven beyond proper care for my family. Fortunately, I saw the problem earlier than most and was able to make corrections.

The same things can happen when men or women use all their extra time for church activities or ministry. If you add career to ministry, the family receives even less time. The Scriptures clearly teach that "no one can serve two masters, for either he will hate the one and love the other, or he will hold to one and despise the other. You cannot serve God and Mammon [riches]" (Matthew 6:24).

Then how much can I give to my job? Here are a few of the common problems to be considered.

Overwork and Overambition

These problems are prevalent in jobs that do not have fixed hours. Some workers tend to drive themselves beyond their physical and emotional limits. A person may be in a job ill-suited to his personality and ability. One frequent error is to try to produce too much in too short a time—to be overly optimistic about what can be accomplished. Jobs that *regularly* require more than fifty hours a week will lead to difficulty in family and ministry.

I Like My Job Too Much

Some people enjoy their work so much that it is almost recreation for them. But such an obsession with work can lead to excessive time away from home and to resenting any other activities. In my second year in the Air Force, I was assigned to Cape Kennedy as a mission controller. That was during the heyday of space, and the job was tremendously interesting. I gave it everything I had—working late nights and occasionally all night. Coupled with many Christian activities, it meant that I left home before my son awoke and came home after he went to bed. This went on for two years of his life. I was clearly neglecting my family. God had to get my attention in a rather severe way. I then spent the next two years winning my son back. This took an entire reorientation of my priorities.

If you are one who loves your work, guard your time well. Take extra precautions to spend time with your family and to have a spiritual outreach.

> ▶Do I have extra work because I am not getting my regular work done? Can I concentrate and accomplish more in the regular time?
> ▶Am I working overtime just for the impression it makes on people?
> ▶Have I simply gotten into a habit of working extra hours?
> ▶Is the extra work unnecessary?

If your answer to any of these questions is yes, you are the basic cause of the overtime and should make some immediate adjustments. If the overtime is necessary on an extended basis, try these steps:

1. Keep a record of what you do for two or three weeks.
2. Take that record and discuss the situation with your supervisor to try to reduce the overtime. Make suggestions that will help him solve the problems instead of throwing all the burden of a solution on him.
3. If there is no way to change the situation, you must decide if you really want to continue in that job, since this may be God's way of directing you toward other employment.

In this process do *not* try to avoid all overtime. Extra hours are a legitimate part of your responsibility as a salaried employee. You simply want to avoid excessive, continuing overtime.

Pressure to Produce
Many jobs carry a great deal of pressure—especially if there is a commission or a quota. This can drain both emotions and time, especially if a person is not particularly capable in the job. In this instance, ask God for special ability to perform and be able to relax in the midst of pressure. Not everyone is emotionally built for this kind of job.

Jobs Beyond Your Ability, Training, or Capacity
Each of us has limits, even in tasks for which we are trained or have experience. Our ability will have limits, or we may have some native ability but not the proper training. When we have both the ability and the training, we may not have the capacity (how much we can accomplish in a given time) for the job.

When you neither recognize your limits, nor admit them, nor take action, you may work excessive overtime to catch up or learn. Even then you may not do the job right or well. You should let your boss know when you are unable to do the work. In most cases, he will appreciate your honesty, since he wants the work done well. If you remain silent, you will in effect be lying to your boss by allowing him to assume you are qualified. This does not mean that you should never take risks or stretch yourself in new areas, but it does mean you should be direct with your superiors and ask for the training or help you need. Certainly the boss does not want the backhoe digging up a gas line or a cost overrun due to incorrect bidding. Combine a "can do" spirit with good judgment and honesty.

How much can you give to a job? All the effort and quality rightfully expected of you to earn your wages—and a little more beyond that. When there is a *legitimate* need for a *short time*, give it all the extra time and effort necessary. Never fail your employer when he needs help. Be reliable in emergencies, but do not "sell your soul to the company store."

At one point in my career I was working in the Pentagon. Everyone arrived in the office early, before the general, and did not leave until he left, which was often well into the evening. There really wasn't extra work to do, and nothing significant was accomplished during that extra time. It was simply part of a system that had built up: be there when the general was there. I decided I would arrive and leave at the stated times unless there was a special need. I finished all my work in that period. However, I can recall that when we had a real need, I worked right on through the night to get the job done.

NOTES: 1. *Bits & Pieces* (Fairfield, N.J.: The Economics Press, January 1981), pages 1-4.

2. Adam Smith, *The Money Game* (New York: Random House, 1967), page 14.

3. Richard C. Halverson, *Perspective*, Volume XXXV, Number 2 (McLean, Va.: Concern Ministries, Inc., January 19, 1983).

4. Howard Butt, *The Velvet Covered Brick* (New York: Harper & Row, 1973), page 125.

Chapter Eight

LIFE CRISES

M.◆ Scott Peck begins his best-selling book, *The Road Less Traveled*, with the statement, "Life is difficult."[1] It is true. Life is filled with one difficult issue after another. To believe otherwise is to live in a fantasy world.

Often those crises involve work. But work cannot be exempt from the rest of one's life. That would violate a basic thesis of this book. All of life must be treated as a whole.

In our earlier work, *The Christian in Mid-Life*, we identified many issues that emerge with force in mid-life. But later we saw that age was a minor part of the problem. They were really "life" crises.

At the beginning of a four-week seminar we asked people to share their typical *feelings* and *responses* to a crisis. The group consisted of thirty-one men and women between the ages of thirty-five and fifty-seven. They were from varied backgrounds—married, single, and divorced. Here are some of their responses:

▶ Free-floating anxiety
▶ Frustration

▶ A lack of purpose or direction, even when purpose and direction had been obvious earlier

▶ Isolation: the sense of being alone, with no one who cares or can help

▶ A changed self-concept: sudden shifts in my view of my ambition and potential

▶ Feelings of worthlessness: the suspicion that I no longer have a contribution to make and my usefulness has ended

▶ Feelings of being trapped: the claustrophobia of life, when I think there is no way out—either at work or in marriage

▶ Lust: a new tendency to consider mental and physical infidelity

▶ A declining sexual drive for no apparent reason

▶ Fear about financial matters that never bothered me before

▶ Realizing the universality of growing older and its accompanying lack of health, stamina, and opportunities

▶ Weariness and fatigue: a sense of constantly being tired, but not from obvious age or health problems

▶ Self-centered sympathy: feeling I'm getting a "raw deal" or that people don't understand me

▶ Rebellion in areas I once accepted calmly

▶ Giving up: an overwhelming temptation to quit a task, a job, a project, or a marriage

▶ Depression: an empty, unexplainable feeling of being down emotionally

▶ Boredom with things that once were stimulating

▶ Anger over issues and incidents I once tolerated

▶ Bitterness: an anger against people or situations

▶ Hopelessness: the feeling that no matter what I do the situation will not improve

▶Easily surfaced emotions: crying with little provocation

▶Feeling I will "explode": the internal pressure that makes me feel I am about to have a nervous breakdown

This is a grim list. Just reading it makes us feel depressed. Yet, this list reflects reality for many people—Christians and nonChristians. These feelings are real, laced with a depth of hurt rarely expressed to others. They usually smolder and ferment until they boil over with a damaging blow to marriage, health, or career.

These feelings are complex, caused by no single incident or background; consequently the feelings can't be changed by simple answers. But there are roots and reasons—and answers. Definite help can be found in Scripture and in a personal relationship with Jesus Christ. He is Lord over our feelings as well as our circumstances.

TRANSITION AND CHANGE

Crisis situations can occur at any age. For sake of discussion, let's look at the age issue as it relates to transition and change. Age creeps up on us with no possibility of reversal or slowing down. We cannot turn back the clock, even for a second.

Age is change—small changes, large changes, slow changes, imperceptible changes—but always change. Learning to live with change and transition is a major issue in coping with life.

In one sense, all of life is a transition from one age to another. Over time the changes are distinct enough that we can classify life into general age categories, as in this arrangement:

Childhood	0-12
Adolescence	13-20
Young adult	21-35
Mid-life	35-55
Mature adulthood	55-70
Elderly	70 and older

Daniel Levinson uses slightly different age boundaries but further defines certain year groups as "transition" stages. He calls seventeen to twenty-two the early adult transition, forty to forty-five the mid-life transition, fifty to fifty-five the age fifty transition, and sixty to sixty-five the late adult transition.

In addition to increasing age there is another key indicator of life crises—*events*. Certain events provide major transitions in life that can very often stimulate emotional responses just as strongly as does age. These events are often the first occurrences of certain dramatic changes in our lives—job, marriage, children, and divorce. A typical sequence of these events would be:

High school to college (or job)
College (or high school) to job
Job change
Marriage
Children
Divorce (Divorce is so common that it must be included, though we don't condone it.)
Teenage children
Career change
Illness
The "empty nest"
Menopause
Retirement

All these transitions evoke emotional responses and drains. But when do these events generally occur? Look at the chart below.

AGE		EVENT
Childhood	0-12	
Adolescence	13-20	High school to college or job
		College to job
		Job change
Young adult	21-35	Marriage
		Children
		Divorce
		Teenage children
Mid-life	35-55	Career change
		Illness
		The empty nest
		Menopause
Mature adulthood	55-70	Retirement
Elderly	70 and older	

Notice the tremendous concentration of emotionally draining events frequently occurring in mid-life. Do you still wonder why stress appears there? Just at the time when sinking roots and settling down begins to seem attractive, compelling changes invade and overturn our plans.

Every change—a new job, a move, a child leaving home, being fired, or a divorce—has the potential of setting off a crisis.

But, as we will see, crises can be avoided—and especially shortened. Our tolerance for change can be developed by learning to be more flexible. If we resist change in our twenties, how can we ever expect anything other than rigidity and inflexibility in our thirties and forties? Change is the price of life or the strife of life—depending on your viewpoint. Welcomed, it serves and develops. Feared and resisted, it petrifies and shatters.

Should life be different for Christians? Yes. Is life automatically different for Christians? No. Do most Christians handle life's problems better than nonChristians? Unfortunately, no. Being a Christian is purported to make us happier and to solve our problems. But this doesn't seem so for many.

The reason? Many people *are* Christians but they do not apply Christian truth and practice to their lives. They think, live, and act like nonChristians and so they reap the same results. But Christians do have resources that are unavailable to nonChristians, if they will but use them.

"They will still bear fruit in old age, they will stay fresh and green" (Psalm 92:14, NIV). This verse reflects the desire of every Christian. We do not want to simply survive in life. We want to engage triumphantly in a life of new fruitfulness and increased usefulness to God.

Consider these fundamental resources a Christian has that a nonChristian does not:

The Christian possesses eternal life (see John 5:25). This eternal life is not only a future experience beyond death. It begins now for all of life. Many people simply "assume" they are Christians because they are church attenders or members, or because they live a moral, upright life. But that is not what makes a person a Christian. We become acutely aware of our need for God as we encounter problems beyond our control. We may pray and go to church more regularly, but feel that our prayers are bouncing off the ceiling.

This may be the time to make sure you have actually understood the gospel and become a true Christian. The first step in becoming a Christian is to realize and admit you have sinned and have no hope of eternal life unless this sin is forgiven. "For all have sinned and fall short of the glory of God" (Romans 3:23). The results of this sin are described in Romans 6:23—"For the wages of sin is death, but the free gift of God is eternal life in Christ Jesus our Lord." Even though we have sinned, God provided a way to eternal life through Jesus Christ.

This eternal life comes by asking Jesus Christ to be one's Savior and Lord—a conscious decision based on the facts of Scripture. By this step of faith, a person acknowledges that *only* through Christ's deity, death, and resurrection can one become a Christian and have eternal life. This is no trivial matter. If how to become a Christian is not clear to you, we suggest further study of the Bible, especially in the Gospel of John. Personal salvation establishes the foundation for dealing with every crisis of life.[2]

The Christian possesses the Holy Spirit. Jesus said, "I will ask the Father, and he will give you another Counselor to be with you forever—the Spirit of truth" (John 14:16-17, NIV). This Counselor is the Holy Spirit. He is the empowering force in our lives. When we fall into difficult circumstances, the Holy Spirit gives us power to endure. He gives enlightenment as we read the Scriptures and guidance on how to live. "But when He, the Spirit of truth, comes, He will guide you into all the truth" (John 16:13).

NonChristians have no access to this inner spiritual power. They must depend only on their own minds and wills to face life. Regrettably, many Christians do not take advantage of the power available to them, but rather rely on unChristian ways of living and thinking.

Christians can claim promises like 2 Peter 1:3 (NIV):

"His divine power has given us everything we need for life and godliness through our knowledge of him who called us by his own glory and goodness." God has provided power for every situation—real power, not just a mystical fantasy or theory. The key to tapping God's power is obedience. Obey God's Word. Apply its principles to your life today.

The Christian possesses the Word of God, the Bible. "All Scripture is inspired by God and profitable for teaching, for reproof, for correction, for training in righteousness" (2 Timothy 3:16). The Bible contains the answer for every problem a person faces. But doesn't a nonChristian have the same resource? Only in a limited sense. A nonChristian can apply the principles of the Bible, but it will not have power since the Scriptures have never been activated by receiving Christ. The Word of God is a never-ending reserve for guidance and direction, but a closed Bible cannot help. We must delve into it, search out its depths, and apply it to our lives. Answers are not simply a cookbook recipe, nor is the Bible simply an answer book. Through the illuminating power of the Holy Spirit we can discover truth that will revolutionize our lives.

CRISIS INDICATORS FOR WOMEN

In case you had not noticed, men and women are different—in spite of attempts to mold a unisex view of life, especially in the workplace. Thus we experience unique sets of issues that ignite crises for men and women.

With some idea of possible transitions or problems to expect in their lives, women can more readily prepare to meet them with a godly perspective. These times can be an invaluable opportunity for God to draw them into a sweeter relationship with Himself and to mold their characters into the image of Jesus Christ.

Appearance

What can be more startling to a woman of forty than to unexpectedly see her relaxed reflection in a mirror? Her jumbled thoughts ask, "Does my stomach really sag? Why does my hair look so dull? Why had I never noticed the deep wrinkles around my mouth? Is that a double chin as well?"

We see what we want to see. We may notice wrinkles around our eyes, but that isn't so bad because the jaw line is still firm. What if the waistline is a little thick? Just standing a little straighter camouflages that.

Many women rationalize, ignore, or resent the changes in their appearance rather than accepting them as one of the marks of God's gift of years. If you are skeptical about the changes in your once youthful appearance, attend a class reunion. Women you haven't seen for ten or twenty years will look distinctly older—wrinkled, heavy, sagging, and gray. A few will still retain their smooth skin and firm figures, but they have probably done so with considerable effort and expense.

Our society places an inordinate emphasis on physical attractiveness. As Dr. James Dobson says, "Without question, the most highly valued personal attribute in our culture (and most others) is physical attractiveness."[3] Any woman who varies from the ideal of beauty automatically loses esteem among her peers.

We should outgrow such standards as we mature, but unfortunately we haven't. Retailers cater as much to the middle-aged as to the young. We see stores with well-stocked cosmetic counters, numerous exercise clubs, cosmetic surgeons (almost three dozen in our city alone), bulging clothes racks in fashionably stocked stores, and dozens of magazines devoted to beautifying the human body.

Advertisers want women to believe they will be disliked and shunned if they have a few flakes of dandruff on the collar, one tiny liver spot on the hand, a sag in their panty hose, or any trace of a wrinkle or blemish. We know, at least intellectually, that "the LORD looks at the heart" but the fact that "man looks at the outward appearance" (1 Samuel 16:7) colors our thinking.

Christian women seek to beautify themselves just as others do. And Christian women do have a responsibility to appear as attractive and as well-groomed as time and finances permit. But they also need the spiritual and personal maturity to accept the aging process as a natural, and yes, a welcome indication of life's progression. This also means accepting others' imperfections as well.

While our family was attending a horseback-riding performance at a state fair, a severely handicapped young man was brought in his wheelchair and placed near the entrance to the grandstand. He was confined to his chair. His hands and face moved with involuntary twitches continuously. But from his clear expression and the interested way he observed the performance, we sensed that he was an intelligent young man.

Many people streamed by him as they were entering or leaving the stadium. After one quick look at the young man, they would glance away and hurry by. Finally another young man came by, wearing broken sandals, torn jeans, and a rumpled shirt, his long hair bound with a rubber band. He alone stopped, smiled, looked directly at the young man, and said, "Hey, how are you today?" before walking on. Although he was careless about his own appearance, he more than all the others who passed by showed that he recognized the worth of the young man in the wheelchair.

A friend of ours recently described a conversation she had with a young couple, Joe and Kathy. Joe frequently made suggestions to Kathy about her hairstyle, clothing, and posture, and often criticized her general appearance. After listening to his stream of criticism, our friend suggested to Joe that he consider the impression he was conveying to his wife. All of his comments focused on her external appearance and not on her inner person.

"What will Kathy do in the years to come when she knows her physical attractiveness is diminishing?" our friend asked. "What will she do when her skin wrinkles and sags? What if she loses a breast to a mastectomy? Or what if her hair turns prematurely gray? She can only assume that your approval and affection will be withdrawn because she has heard only your comments about her physical appearance." Joe accepted the suggestions and began eliminating his criticisms and learning to see his wife as a complete person.

Our appearance will change. No one can nullify the effects of aging. But our response to these changes will determine our inner serenity and self-acceptance.

Health

Shirley is a good friend. After years of serving the Lord on the missionfield and caring for her own children and husband, she was stricken with several illnesses. She had diabetes, then cancer, and finally heart surgery. All were disabling, limiting, difficult illnesses. Her failing health has affected her appearance, her capacity as a wife, mother and homemaker, and her service in her community and church. Yet she cannot change her history and must trust God for the grace to endure.

As we see godly women like Shirley who suffer illness, we develop a greater appreciation for our own health. We realize how fragile our bodies really are, and that our good health may deteriorate at any time.

Women as well as men often fear *serious illness* as they grow older, knowing their increasing vulnerability. It is a natural response to worry that symptoms may suggest a dread disease and fear the consequences, though knowing God is in control.

But women need not be defeated by sickness when it comes. My mother developed a serious degenerative illness and it progressed for several years until her death in her late fifties. The disease gradually reduced her from an able, gifted woman to one who was completely bedridden.

But with the deterioration of her health, a spiritual strength emerged that may never have flourished if God had not limited her physically. She completely accepted the changes and adapted to the circumstances in which God placed her. After a day in bed she once told her husband, "The days pass so quickly. There are so many people to pray for."

If the Lord chooses to allow illness, He also gives us the grace and comfort to accept and adapt. "God is able to make all grace abound to you, so that in all things at all times, having all that you need, you will abound in every good work" (2 Corinthians 9:8, NIV).

Loneliness

One woman said recently: "I feel so alone. I have a lovely home, a faithful husband, an active social life, but I don't know of one person who is really interested in me—what I think, what matters to me, and who I am inside. I feel like I'm living alone, suspended in time, while everyone around me goes on with the business of living."

Many women experience a deep sense of loneliness and isolation. An emphasis on liberation, a proper self-image, fulfillment, and a rewarding career all combine to confuse and isolate many women. Changing social values further complicate these issues. How does a woman discover what will bring her satisfaction and fulfillment? In an attempt to ignore or mask their loneliness, some women develop attitudes of indifference, hostility, or even frivolity and self-indulgence.

Jane, the wife of a successful executive, raised three daughters and kept a lovely home. She was well-known in the community for her activities. But when her daughters left home, she felt empty and lonely. She discovered that although she loved her husband as he loved her, they had allowed years to pass while she concentrated on the children and he majored on his career. They were nominally Christian, preferring to give money to the Lord's work rather than being personally involved.

Jane's sister, Joyce, observed Jane's lonely frustration. Joyce knew God intimately and realized Jane needed a fresh approach to spiritual things. She encouraged Jane to read the Scriptures and pray daily. She then urged her sister to take an interest in other people.

Jane's interests changed as she developed consistent communication with God. She volunteered to teach a girls' Sunday school class—something she had not done since she was in college. She began to love these girls and eagerly anticipated each Sunday with them. She visited them in their homes and even led one girl's mother to Christ.

About a year after Joyce had first confronted her, Jane suddenly realized, "Why, I haven't thought about being lonely for months. Thank You, Lord, and thank you, Joyce."

Anxiety

Many women are apprehensive and uneasy when they face new developments in life. Their anxiety may develop over many years, but it can explode suddenly with devastating results.

A woman may be anxious about her children and the possible harm, spiritual and physical, that they might encounter. Or she may be worried about finances, her husband's interest in her, her aging parents' health and welfare, her own health, problems in her church, the state of the world—anything and everything, both known and unknown.

Anxiety interferes with a woman's relationships and makes it difficult to accomplish tasks, and to plan and schedule. Somehow her mind refuses to concentrate on anything except possible problems.

Someone has said that ninety percent of the things we worry about never happen. If this is true, we waste much of our physical and emotional energy by allowing anxiety to sap our strength, raise our blood pressure, increase our pulse rate, and tense our muscles.

An anxious woman fills her mind with self-doubt and fear. She dreads responsibility and making decisions and, most of all, she dreads her feeling of anxiety.

God has provided communication with Himself as the antidote for anxiety, as Paul wrote in Philippians 4:6: "Be anxious for nothing, but in everything by prayer and supplication with thanksgiving let your requests be made known to God."

Practicing this command to pray requires discipline of the mind and soul—a willingness and readiness to take all our troubles and worries into the presence of God and then concentrate on thanksgiving. The result—inward peace that is unavailable from any other source—protects the mind from renewed attacks of anxiety.

Anger
We can list several issues that can stimulate anger in women:

▶ Lack of appreciation or approval at home or at work
▶ Feeling personally unfulfilled
▶ No career outside the home

▶ Unused gifts and talents
▶ The need to work to provide extra income
▶ Rebellious children
▶ Personal failure
▶ Undeveloped talent
▶ Full schedules
▶ Unreasonable demands from family and friends

Some women feel their opportunities for growth and development in their education, career, or personal ministry are hindered by marriage or age, and they become angry and bitter. In their thirties or forties, they often see a last chance to change their life's direction and to reach out once more for their goals and dreams. If those changes don't come, they seethe with inward resentment that bursts into outward actions ultimately.

Anger manifests itself in many ways:

▶ Lack of love
▶ Aggressiveness
▶ A critical spirit
▶ Malicious speech
▶ Deep, inner bitterness
▶ Hatred
▶ Spiritual coldness

Spiritual maturity helps us recognize anger for what it is—sin—then to confess it and avoid it in the future.

Ultimately all anger is directed toward God because we think He allowed certain events but not others, and therefore didn't arrange things to suit us.

Anger is a dangerous, destructive emotion, both internally and toward others. David wrote in Psalm 37:8 (NIV), "Refrain from anger and turn from wrath; do not fret—it leads only to evil." Paul knew of the devastating results of anger when he wrote in Colossians 3:8, "But now you also, put them all aside: anger, wrath, malice, slander, and abusive speech from your mouth."

Powerlessness

Irreversible events take place—parents die, our health fails, our children rebel, we suffer through an unwanted divorce, or we are fired from a job.

We panic when we feel there is little hope of restoring our former happiness. The years slip away, and we can't force events to meet our expectations. We struggle and manipulate but still seem powerless to change the course of our lives.

I met a woman who seemed locked into impossible circumstances. Her husband, a pastor, left her for another woman. Her children had already left home, her income was meager, and her health was beginning to crumble. Her husband would not return, her children lived their own lives, and her limited training prevented her from changing jobs. She could not keep the pressure from draining her health and stamina.

From time to time we all feel caught in the grip of circumstances or under the control of others. Only a firm conviction that God controls everything can give stability and meaning to such difficult situations.

Spiritual Emptiness

Matthew and Sandy were married for twenty-three years. During that time they were active in their church and the spiritual life of their community. Suddenly Matthew announced he was going to divorce Sandy, move to another state, build a cabin in the mountains, and pursue a writing career. Sandy listened in stunned silence. Matthew's abrupt rejection and unwillingness to consider her pleading for a reconciliation devastated Sandy. For a short time she sought consolation among church friends but found they were awkward and uncomfortable in her presence. In bitter frustration she stopped attending church. She began dating nonChristian men and drifted into an unhappy life of sin.

Was Matthew to blame? Partly. But although Sandy had devoted years of her life to Christian "activities," she had neglected her own spiritual growth and when trials came, she collapsed. She was a spiritual baby.

It's overwhelming to realize that after years of professing to be a Christian, our spiritual exercises can become routine and meaningless, or to see that our growth has been minimal. At a time when we should be helping others we have nothing to give. All we know are dry spells of spiritual indifference and drifting from the things of God.

In churches all across America, women faithfully attend services and participate in women's Bible studies and prayer groups. But often it's only a public performance. Their private walk with God does not match their public display. Certainly they receive blessing and enrichment from the group activities, but all the while they are missing God's very best. If you realize your lack of spiritual depth, don't be discouraged. Be grateful God has given you the insight to recognize your failure. Resolve to begin growing as a disciple of Christ.

Career Problems
Many women are locked in a boring, routine job and long desperately for a challenging career. They feel restless, desiring something more, but unable to find it or to expand their capacities and income.

But anyone who looks for life's fulfillment in a career alone makes a serious mistake. Jobs can be interesting, stimulating, and rewarding; but true fulfillment comes only through a relationship with God and by making a contribution to other people's lives.

The proposition that women can find happiness through a career has led to strong dissatisfaction and resentment on the part of many Christian women.

CRISIS INDICATORS FOR MEN

A man's life motivation and the problems he faces often differ significantly from what a woman must deal with. Career tasks predominate his experiences because he cannot stop functioning as a breadwinner for the family. He thinks he is trapped. He has a sense of being imprisoned, and escape is impossible.

As a man experiences life transitions, he suddenly faces unfamiliar issues. He begins to ask if he chose the right career. He reviews his past and compares it with the dreams and goals he once pursued. He looks at his marriage and wonders why it doesn't meet his expectations. He avoids the mirror, which reveals obvious physical changes. He begins to doubt his abilities and potential. In short, he begins a total reappraisal of his life. But this questioning need not be bad. In fact, failure to go through it may well rob a man of a significant opportunity.

It certainly is not mandatory to have some traumatic crisis. But even when there is no crisis, changes still take place in a man's life and he must respond and adjust to them. He could decline rather than develop, but it need not be so.

Most authorities agree that the major life areas for a man are his career and family—in that order. Others are important, but these two dominate as driving forces. I would add a third area that most secular sources ignore—the spiritual dimension. It is key, for it gives perspective and power. His spiritual life reshapes and refines the basic fabric of a man's existence. Treating career, family, and other areas without a spiritual focus touches only symptoms—relieving the outward pain, but failing to deal with root causes. Life crises must be examined in the context of spiritual development.

Age

I recall an incident that occurred about eight years ago. I had had a good day. The entire family was asleep and the house was cooling with the February night. Mary was asleep beside me. Snug between the sheets and blankets, I was warmly comfortable. It was a good time to think, and I did—about many things. I began reviewing where I was in life. I thought about aging and my next birthday. *Three score and ten years. Well, I have half of my life yet to live.* Then I came alert with a start. *That's not true. I'm almost forty-two—seven years over the halfway mark. Eight more years to my half-century!*

In that moment I realized I had mentally suspended myself at age thirty-five. It was only then I realized I was clinging to youth and not fully recognizing that I was getting older.

But I should have noticed it earlier. That inevitable roll of fat was fighting with my belt for position. Gray hairs then balanced the brown in number. I found myself less daring physically, and muscular aches more pronounced. Being around our teenage children and their friends vividly emphasized my lack of youth.

Yet youth is so hard to give up—even though we have no choice. We live in a youth-oriented culture. A friend in the personnel business recently told me that by the time a man is twenty-six to twenty-nine you can tell if he will make it as an executive. That could be discouraging to one who is long past that age.

Reflecting on age, Henry Still comments,

There comes a day—perhaps a chill, damp dawn in autumn—when it is more difficult to spring out of bed and face the work of the world. You feel a twinge of stiffness in knee or shoulder. Dry skin flakes when you scratch. Sitting on the edge of the bed, reluctant to meet the day, you contemplate blue veins on ankle or calf and brown pigment spots on the back of your hand.

There has been a change in the weather, you note absently, signaled by soreness in the pink slash of scar where the gallbladder came out last year. Dawn provides a moment to wonder how high your blood pressure is today and the cholesterol. You can't quite remember what it was you told yourself last night not to forget this morning.

A bathroom mirror is cruel at dawn. It reveals a roll of fat around the body, loose skin under the chin, and gray in the stubble before the lather goes on.[4]

The realization that our youth is slipping away startles many of us to varied emotional reactions. Some are fearful. Others push and work harder. Some try to dress and act young. Some exercise frantically. Many give up. But all inevitably lose the battle and crash into mid-life—perhaps kicking and screaming against its pull.

In the midst of a major reappraisal of his life, a man with a proper perspective will emerge as a new man. Yet the turmoil of the time will often confuse him. As Daniel Levinson aptly observes,

For the great majority of men . . . this period evokes tumultuous struggles within the self and with the external world. Their Mid-Life Transition is a time of moderate or severe crisis. Every aspect of their lives comes into question, and they are horrified by much that is revealed. They are full of recriminations against themselves and others. They cannot go on as before, but need time to choose a new path or modify the old one.

Because a man in this crisis is often somewhat irrational, others may regard him as "upset" or "sick." In most cases, he is not. The man himself and those who care about him should recognize that he is in a normal developmental period and is working on normal mid-life tasks. The desire to question and modify his life stems from the most healthy part of the self. The doubting and searching are appropriate to this period; the real question is how to best make use of them.[5]

There is hope. There are solutions for the countless problems that spring up with age. These problems had their roots in a man's earlier years, but develop fully in the fertile ground of physical and emotional changes in later years.

And just as his decisions in late adolescence and early adulthood influenced his life for the coming decades, so now what he does will determine his lifestyle for the next twenty or thirty years. His decisions now will greatly affect his career, his marriage, and his eventual fulfillment in retirement. He must not pass up the opportunity to grow, or ignore the reality of the pain felt in the process of growing.

Career
I once had a discussion with an Air Force colonel during his last assignment before he retired at about age forty-five. I asked what he planned to do after retirement. His reply startled me: "My problem is that I haven't really decided what to do when I grow up." I laughed, but his statement was

a perceptive one for a man of his age.

Growth is the key. It is imperative for a man not to sense he has been embalmed and buried in his job. He must see growth—in pay, variety of work, benefits, position, and recognition. But even with growth, he may still feel unfruitful and unmotivated in his career.

A man's identity is welded to his job. After the question, "What is your name?" another follows almost invariably, "What do you do?" We categorize and pigeonhole people by their work, especially men. A carpenter, a lawyer, a doctor, a draftsman, an engineer, a factory worker—all conjure up a mental picture of the person. From this picture a man builds his self-image and tends to become what he and others expect him to be.

We can agree that this process is wrong. The personality and worth of a man is not derived from his job, but from his character. Certainly this is true in God's sight.

Consider the typical history of a man's work. In his teens he alternately dreams about and dreads working on his own. In his late teens and early twenties he prepares by experience and education. Often he takes a shot in the dark, for how can he know what he really wants to do? So he propels himself out into a career.

In his twenties he becomes totally independent of his family, begins developing in his job, and may start a family of his own. It is a hectic time of change and preoccupation with finding his place in the world. He may return to school, change jobs, or even fail at something. Yet he may experience little emotional turmoil because the resiliency of youth carries him through.

He generally enters his life's work by his late twenties or early thirties and aggressively pursues promotion, pay raises, or other kinds of security, reward, and stability in life. To this point his career still dominates his thinking, with some emphasis on his family and marriage.

Then by thirty-five or forty, several things begin to happen. A man now knows himself well enough to perceive (though perhaps not admit to himself) that his job future is limited in terms of promotion, success, and creativity. He is no longer a "promising young man." He is now expected to pull his own weight and produce. He may be bound by limitation in his ability or education. Yet he is keenly aware of his need to concentrate on "making it," as Levinson says, by achieving something in the way of position, comfort, or security.

If his struggle to this point has been financial, the pursuit of security will be most important. If finances have been adequate, comfort and position dominate. In his mind there is some kind of ladder that he must climb. Levinson describes this ladder as "all dimensions of advancement—increases in social rank, income, power, fame, creativity, quality of family life, social contribution—as these are important for the man and his world." The result is a striving "to become a senior member in one's world, to speak more strongly with one's own voice, and to have a greater measure of authority."[6]

In many jobs the remaining rungs on the ladder disappear. There is no place left to climb. In other jobs the ladder is there, but a man lacks the ability or drive to climb it. Or his job may be boring or unfulfilling, or marred by conflicting relationships. In either case a sense of failure and despair emerges. The stark realization of limitations initiates a crisis.

Other work-related factors that may signal a crisis include a wounded pride, a sense of failure, and financial insecurity.

Wounded pride. "Pride goes before destruction, and a haughty spirit before stumbling" (Proverbs 16:18). Wounded pride can easily drive a man to some form of depression. When he finds he has limitations or that his potential is at an end, his ego will be hurt. But he does not like to admit his pride or be confronted with it in his job. He may tend to overrate his youthfulness and build an unfounded level of pride. But reality will later shatter his assessment.

Failure. No one is totally successful in everything he does. Failure is common to every man. Not making the basketball team in high school may be a severe blow to an athletically-minded teenager. Not being accepted by a particular university can also be a painful failure to some degree. But in the key areas of family and career, failure is particularly distressing for a man who is beyond his youth.

Yet failure is one of the chisels that God uses to shape a man into His image for greater use later. Many men go through their early adult life scrambling for success at any price instead of balancing career goals with family and personal needs. Consequently, they pay a high price for success. An initial sense of fulfillment soon gives way to emptiness when they realize they have failed with their family or in the personal dimension of their lives.

For most men, a life crisis will coincide with a sense of failure at work—perhaps as minor as a delayed promotion, a gentle reprimand, or a missed opportunity; or as great as being fired, rebuked, or obviously surpassed by younger men. Demands for excessive overtime or being given tasks beyond their ability can also contribute to a sense of failure. But whatever the failure, it must be evaluated in the context of the total experience at that point in their life.

Paul could well have sensed failure in his mission as he wrote to Timothy from prison:

At my first defense no one supported me, but all deserted me. . . . But the Lord stood with me, and

strengthened me, in order that through me the procla-
mation might be fully accomplished, and that all the
Gentiles might hear; and I was delivered out of the
lion's mouth. (2 Timothy 4:16-17)

Paul clearly saw that God's purposes were being accomplished even in discouraging circumstances.

Failure may be the very thing that causes a man to
reassess his entire life structure and future. It also drives us to
God and fosters a new dependence on Him, as expressed in
Psalm 119:67,71: "Before I was afflicted I went astray, but
now I keep Thy word. . . . It is good for me that I was
afflicted, that I may learn Thy statutes."

Financial uncertainty. Financial pressures can force a
man to stay on a job he detests and keep him from starting
out in a new life direction. They can make him compromise
his standard of ethics to keep his job. They can precipitate
family arguments and turmoil. The pressure to maintain or
increase his level of income can make a man feel trapped in a
career at a time when he most desires a change. Even the man
who draws a large salary generally spends it all or takes risks
in investments that produce the pressure of uncertainty and
anxiety.

Other factors in work may signal a life crisis for a man.
Issues like interpersonal conflict, pressure to produce,
demands to move or quit, pressure to work excessive overtime, tasks beyond his ability or career, dissatisfaction, and
boredom all may strike an open nerve and produce a crisis
situation. And, for a man, it will be a pivotal point of his life.

The first step in coping with a career-related crisis is to
avoid impulsive moves. Instead, give careful thought to
rebuilding your life's structure and goals. Concentrate on
basic values and issues, not on feelings and incidents. Give
the highest priority to revising your spiritual foundations.

Marriage and the Family

Several years ago I took my family on a camping vacation in California. Just before we left home, my company underwent a sudden change in management with the subsequent likelihood of reorganization. Most probably I would be asked to move to a new location. The vacation was a noticeable progression from one phone booth to another as I kept abreast of developments. I was unable to sleep at night—a rare occurrence for me. Thoughts, ideas, and deep emotions kept me unsettled, but not about my job or our possible move. I was disturbed about how little time I had left with my son, who was then in high school, and how many things I had failed to do for him and with him. I was troubled.

After a couple of nights of turmoil, I sat down in a forest campground in California and wrote out my thoughts. I made some plans and commitments. Then I was totally at peace and we continued our vacation. In my case, a possible change of job circumstances highlighted a need in my family and caused me to reevaluate my priorities and lifestyle.

Most men choose wives who can share their dreams of the future. Their marriage begins on an idealistic note, but reality sets in as the struggle of marital adjustment ensues. If the marriage survives the early tests, stability usually prevails for several years. Then another reassessment process begins that can lead to severe conflict and crisis. Some aspects of this reassessment impinge especially on the man.

Lust. Sexual lust is a special force that can create a spiritual and marital crisis of destructive proportions. If a husband and wife have poor communication and an unsatisfying sexual relationship, the man begins looking around and finds himself tempted by other women who meet the picture of his fantasies. As uncertain feelings and a changing self-image develop, he is more vulnerable to sexual promiscuity and marital infidelity. Many men try to escape through pornography or X-rated films, which simply heighten their dissatisfaction. It is imperative to be aware of the invasion of lust and put up a special guard against it.

Combined with decreasing job satisfaction, a so-so marriage, and a new need to prove himself, the temptation of infidelity can overcome a man. With a sense of abandon and desperation, some men (Christians and nonChristians alike) form illicit relationships to build their wounded egos.

Frequently this process begins when a female friend listens as a man describes his inner struggles. Unfortunately, a few moments of such indiscretion can lead to tragic changes in marriage, reputation, and spiritual influence. Many godly, spiritually mature men have fallen to this temptation only to find that its sweetness and satisfaction turned into bitterness, depression, and a ruined life and marriage.

Divorce. An increasing number of divorces occur as men struggle to discover new goals and achievements. Reasoning, logic, and even love cannot persuade them to stick it out and work through difficulties.

In the United States, half of all marriages end in divorce. Christian marriages have been spared somewhat in the past, but this is rapidly changing. More and more Christians are bailing out of their marriages. They admit it is wrong, but refuse to keep their commitment to seeing their problems through. The tragic result is that children are irreparably hurt as innocent bystanders caught in the backlash of adult irresponsibility.

As the spiritual head of the family, the husband is primarily responsible for taking the lead in reconciliation rather than taking the easy route of divorce.

Physical Changes
He ruffles through the Yellow Pages intent on finding something, not knowing quite where to look. "Gymnasiums,

Sports, Weight—ah, there it is: Health Clubs." He joins one. He chooses clothes that make him look thinner and sportier. He dons jewelry and loosens the top buttons of his shirt. He tries to be tanned earlier and longer. Like many of us, he clings to a more youthful image as he gets older.

What attitude should characterize the Christian man as he grows older? Should he "let himself go"? Should he ignore his age and keep living the life of a young man? Should he adopt vain habits and artifices to cover up? Let's look at the major physical issues and then consider a few suggestions for coping with the changing physical body.

Appearance. Most men over thirty-five find themselves almost constantly engaged in "the battle of the bulge." In our well-fed society, men who do not face this battle are rare. Even those who never previously faced the problem of being overweight will see fat appear on each side of their waist. Excess weight can be controlled by exercise and diet. But it is disconcerting to even the most secure man to see it develop. Ignored, it can lead to a severe weight problem and possibly other health concerns.

I have often caught myself staring remorsefully in the mirror at my waist. My eyes—and my pride, unfortunately—focus on the extra roll of fat there. Although I hate it, I'm not sure I hate it enough to permanently cut back those eight pounds I know I do not need. Yet a mixture of pride and my need for discipline remind me that I am getting older and that habits I develop now will control much of my later life.

But a change in a man's waistline is simply one of many physical changes taking place. Gray starts to invade his hair or his hair begins to fall out—or both. His face begins to lose its youthful smoothness and texture. His muscles become soft. Youth cannot be retrieved.

Energy and endurance. A man's decreasing energy and strength can be even more distressing than changes in his appearance. After thirty a man's body is simply not as resilient as it once was. The attempt to "burn the candle at both ends" results in continuous fatigue and illness, whereas before a good night's rest seemed to repair the entire body system.

This decrease in energy and strength especially affects those whose work includes much physical labor. Carpenters, plumbers, dockworkers, farmers, and many others may care little about their physical appearance, but are greatly affected by decreasing strength because their livelihood depends on it. Sadly, many employers care little about a man's age and physical condition. Often they demand the same amount of work and output from the fifty-year-old as the twenty-five-year-old.

As a man grows older, he must take extra care to remain healthy and in good physical condition or his energy reserves will drop drastically low. Many men find themselves too tired after a day's work to be involved in anything else. Their spiritual outreach, family life, and the sexual relationship in marriage all suffer.

Even though energy and physical strength decrease as we grow older, another resource often increases—endurance. The youth spends his energy in vigorous rushes of activity and soon wears out. But endurance is staying power—the ability to keep going under adverse conditions. It involves physical strength and energy, but also, more importantly, mental and emotional stamina. And these come from experience.

Now we must direct our energies. It is possible to be far more effective than we ever were in our youth, when our energy was often spent inefficiently. It is the wise use of one's energy that counts.

Panic about success. The majority of life crises in men are directly related to their careers. One of the first indicators for a man that a life transition is impending is a panicky desire to succeed. This may be evidenced by a sense of approaching failure, a realization that he has "peaked out," a feeling that time is running out to "make it" in the job, being passed over for some promotion, or feeling an extraordinary pressure to produce. The result of his feelings is an urge to work harder and a fear that his job or career is jeopardized.

External evidences of a crisis are longer working hours, giving the job priority over everything else, neglecting the family and spiritual matters because of "having" to work, and nervousness or irritability with coworkers. The root of this panic is the underlying fear of failure.

Lack of motivation. Another indicator of a possible crisis is a growing lack of motivation in a man's career. This is the opposite reaction to being panicked to succeed. This lack of drive appears mainly on the job, but spills over into other areas of life such as family involvements and spiritual and physical fitness.

A man experiencing this must ask himself, "What motivates me?" His motivation may be wrongly derived from promotion, money, power, or success; and because these are ultimately without significant value, they will eventually disappoint him. But the worthwhile motivation that stems from the desire to support one's family, contribute to a worthy cause, or to influence other men towards a relationship with Jesus Christ, will continue even when job circumstances change.

Fear. An onslaught of fears can be another signal. A man may fear financial or other failure, losing a job, or his children becoming rebellious. Similarly, an unusual focus on security can make a man bury himself in a job that smothers him. Should he lose it, he knows that he may not be quickly hired elsewhere.

Crises are the norm of life. We need to recognize them,

accept them, and realize that they provide great opportunity for growth—or great opportunity for failure.

NOTES: 1. M. Scott Peck, *The Road Less Traveled* (New York: Simon & Schuster/Touchstone Books, 1978).

2. For further information we recommend: *How to Be Born Again*, by Billy Graham (Waco, Tex.: Word, Inc., 1977), and *Basic Christianity*, by John R. W. Stott (Grand Rapids: Eerdmans Publishing Co., 1974).

3. James Dobson, *Hide or Seek* (Old Tappan, N.J.: Fleming H. Revell Co., 1974), page 15.

4. Henry Still, *Man-Made Men* (New York: Hawthorn Books, 1973), pages 178-179.

5. Daniel J. Levinson, *The Seasons of a Man's Life* (New York: Alfred A. Knopf, 1978), page 199.

6. Levinson, *The Seasons of a Man's Life*, pages 59-60.

Chapter Nine

SUCCESS AND FAILURE

Noticing the new colonel's insignia on Tom's shoulders, I congratulated him. But after a few minutes of conversation I said, "Tom, you don't seem too happy about your promotion and new assignment."

"I'm not," he replied. "I tried to resign, but the Air Force refused my resignation."

Unknown to me, Tom's life was falling apart.

Outwardly he was a success. A full colonel in the Air Force. A Ph.D. in Aeronautics. A command pilot with thousands of hours flying time. A Naval Academy graduate. Deputy Commander of a significant Air Force scientific research organization.

But inwardly he despaired. He would drive home from work at Wright-Patterson Air Force Base in Dayton, Ohio, and then sit in his driveway for twenty to thirty minutes trying to analyze where he had gone wrong. Work was depressing. The challenge was gone. Even his fine family was not enough.

As Tom told me later, "All that should have made me happy did no good at all. It seemed I had no friends—at least no one who really cared for me and was concerned about what I was going through."

Eventually Tom did resign from the Air Force and joined a consulting firm. A few months later his daughter Carol told her parents she had committed her life to Jesus Christ after attending a church where she heard an explanation of how to become a Christian. Tom was unmoved, but Carol told him if he ever wanted to experience Christ's living presence he should attend the church she had visited.

Four weeks later Tom's son, an outstanding gymnast, fell and broke his hip. The doctors subsequently found a tumor so large they decided his leg should be amputated just below the buttock.

"I was paralyzed," Tom told me. "My first thought was that I needed God. I remembered what Carol had said, so the following Sunday I went to her church. We were really hurting and needed help. It seemed like the sermon was just for me. It was the first time I had been in a Christ-centered church and experienced God's presence."

Tom returned to the church the next Sunday, and the pastor explained how to become a Christian. Tom prayed that Christ would enter his life and give him salvation.

Meanwhile his son was undergoing further examinations, and the doctors decided to try an operation that might save his leg. He could expect to be in a cast for several months and never compete in gymnastics again.

The operation was successful, and his son's recovery miraculous. His cast was off in seven weeks, and he was back in gymnastics a few months later—going on to win state honors in high school and earning a college athletic scholarship. Furthermore, he had become a Christian through the witness of a friend in the hospital. Tom and his son began doing daily Bible study together.

"All that struggle after achieving worldly success now

makes sense," Tom said. "I had been giving myself to the wrong things. My crisis led me to Christ."

For Tom, an overwhelming sense of failure and need led to the discovery of true success.

Not everyone responds to failure so positively. A newspaper article tells of a man who held a responsible position with a good company. He was on his way up and seemed to have the world by the tail. He acted boldly and exuded confidence. But one day his boss called him into his office and fired him.

He subsequently obtained a good job with better pay. But one year after being fired he described it like this:

"I'd like to be able to tell you that it was a learning experience, and that I'll laugh about it some day, but I can't. I want you to know that it's the closest thing to dying I ever expect to feel. That's the only way to describe it to you. It feels like you're dying.

"I always used to just assume that everyone envied me because of the success I'd had in my work. Now, on paper, I'm just as successful—more successful monetarily—but because of that one blot of being fired, I seem to think that I'm a failure forever and I'm afraid of people finding out. . . .

"Something inside me is saying that if I let loose and enjoy myself too much, I'm going to be yanked back to reality by being fired again. So in a lot of ways I'm not the same person. I'm working and I have a good job, but I'm not the same person. It's only been a year. Maybe it will go away. I don't know."[1]

In the world of work we do face ambition and ability crises—and the possibility of success or failure. No one likes to fail. Everyone wants to succeed. But both success and failure are fraught with danger and temptation if not handled properly. Failure can cause a person to give up and quit and to blame God for the circumstances. Success can inflate the ego and cause people to neglect God. But under God's direction, both success and failure can build us into more mature men and women.

Of course, success is a matter of perspective and attitude. Getting a $50-per-month pay raise may be considered a failure because others got a $100 raise. Or it could be a success because six other employees were laid off.

We have a mania for success in our culture. We exalt the successful athlete, businessman, actor, or politician. We avoid the seeming failures. The theologian A.W. Tozer aptly wrote,

> In this world men are judged by their ability to do. They are rated according to the distance they have come up the hill of achievement. At the bottom is utter failure, at the top complete success; and between these two extremes the majority of civilized men sweat and struggle from youth to old age. . . .
>
> But in all of this there is no happiness. . . .
>
> This mania to succeed is a good thing perverted. The desire to fulfill the purpose for which we were created is of course a gift from God, but sin has twisted this impulse about and turned it into a selfish lust for first place and top honors. By their lust the whole world of mankind is driven as by a demon and there is no escape.[2]

How does God measure success? What does He want for us? He told Joshua if he meditated continually on God's law and carefully observed it, "then you will make your way prosperous, and then you will have success" (Joshua 1:8). Success for us as well is conditional on obedience to God's Word. This is success as seen from God's perspective, not the world's.

As human beings, we usually determine success in one of three ways. The first is merely the *feeling* of having succeeded. Our criteria may be vague and uncertain, yet we can sense something within even though we may be entirely wrong. Our feeling of success may have to do with specific standards or expectations or goals we have set and now judge ourselves by, but these aims could well be unrealistic or unnecessary.

Second, we assess success or failure by *how others judge us*, or how we think they judge us. Again, this evaluation method can be wrong. Judgments by others can be as subjective and unrelated to fact as our own.

Third, *a fixed, unbiased source* can reveal our success: standardized tests, written criteria for promotion or pay raises, or requirements for an educational degree.

But ultimately, God is our only judge. His perspective on our success is the only one that counts. Our feelings, the opinions of others, and fixed standards can never overrule God's values.

OUR VULNERABLE AREAS

Each of us can identify areas of life where success or failure is most important to us, although these can change as we grow older. Five areas that receive the most emphasis among men and women are career, marriage, children, other personal relationships, and our spiritual condition.

The world most often judges success first in the realm of career. Christians often have identical standards as non-Christians in this area, and so they frequently miss success in other equally important ways.

Failure in marriage is more emotionally upsetting than failure in any other area of life. The commitment we make at the outset involves every facet of our life and being. A marriage relationship either grows and develops through the years or it deteriorates and leaves scars.

A middle-aged Christian man who had recently divorced his wife wrote to me about the aftermath: "I guess I've had the normal ups and downs. It has been lonely at times. I also keep re-examining things—still trying to figure out what went wrong. At this point in time, I feel an acute sense of failure in probably one of the most important areas of life."

Divorce rips us apart emotionally and spiritually. Yet Christian couples have every resource and reason to succeed in marriage even though the problems become acute.

As parents, much of our feeling of success depends on our children's successes. Our emotions go up and down as they achieve in some areas and fail in others. Elation and despair can race through our emotions all in the span of an hour as we talk with them. We are emotionally vulnerable because we have less and less control over their success and failure as they become increasingly independent and start making decisions on their own—at times in direct opposition to us.

In our personal relationships outside the immediate family, we often tend to stop growing in our ability to relate to others—at just the time when we have a great need for closer friendships.

As for the spiritual realm, there are few greater tragedies than meeting an older Christian with a distinguished appearance and position only to find that he or she is spiritually immature. For true spiritual maturity is the key to coping with the fallout from problems in all other areas. Yet we so easily neglect spiritual development. When we finally discover our need we may feel it is too late to change—though it never is. No Christian should tolerate failure in the area of spiritual growth. We must succeed here.

Our success or failure in all these areas determines our

self-image—the picture we have of ourselves. The picture may be inaccurate, but it is what we see and believe. Most failures and successes actually begin here—we *think* we will fail or succeed in something because of who we imagine we are. Sooner or later our thoughts emerge in reality as fulfilled prophecy.

WHY DOES GOD ALLOW SUCCESS OR FAILURE?

One man is a committed Christian and a competent worker for his company. He allows God to be in charge of his career. Promotion follows promotion until he advances to the company presidency. A second man is also a committed Christian and a competent worker who keeps his focus on God. But he misses promotions, and, in fact, is soon forced to leave his company. Why?

The answers for the seeming inequalities of life are not simple. They are rooted in God's grand purpose for us, something not easily understood by any of us.

But seeing this in the proper perspective first requires taking a look at the significant difference between the world's view of life and God's view of life. Consider the following:

THE WORLD'S VIEW	GOD'S VIEW
The world focuses on money, possessions, and other things that develop a person's comfort, pleasure, and pride.	God focuses on developing the inner character of a person, so that he reflects all the good qualities God Himself possesses.
The world emphasizes a person's outward position, rank, or prestige.	God emphasizes the person— the infinite worth of the individual.

THE WORLD'S VIEW

The world pushes for short-term gain—getting the most out of life now.

The world emphasizes self-centeredness—a selfishness focused on "my" needs.

The world pushes for self-protection by emphasizing financial and physical security.

GOD'S VIEW

God works for a person's long-term gain—what will benefit him for his earthly life and for eternity.

God helps us focus on the needs of others.

God teaches the need for a strong spiritual life, and that His presence with us is our true security.

The contrasts are obvious. God has totally different goals in mind for Christians than the transient good feeling of supposed success. In the Bible we see this as a two-fold purpose: First, He wants to reconcile each person to Himself through Christ's sacrifice for man's sin. Second, He wants to develop each person into Christ's image.

In the Old Testament, God dealt with the nation of Israel much as He does with individuals today. Trials and triumphs were designed by God for a specific purpose. Deuteronomy 8:1-3 (NIV) says,

> Be careful to follow every command I am giving you today, so that you may live and increase and may enter and possess the land that the LORD promised on oath to your forefathers. Remember how the LORD your God led you all the way in the desert these forty years, to humble you and to test you in order to know what was in your heart, whether or not you would keep his commands. He humbled you, causing you to hunger and then feeding you with manna, which neither you

nor your fathers had known, to teach you that man
does not live on bread alone but on every word that
comes from the mouth of the LORD.

These words punctuated two great events of failure and
success. The Israelites had just experienced forty years of
wandering in the wilderness as a result of their leader's
disobedience. All the adults died in the process except
three—Moses, Joshua, and Caleb. Following that experience
comes the incredibly successful invasion of the Promised
Land. At this point God explained the reason for the failure
of the last forty years and the conditions of the impending
success.

Two thoughts leap off the pages of Scripture—*obedience*
and *remembrance*. Of the two, obedience takes precedence.
The Israelites wandered in the wilderness because of their
disobedience. Their future success depended on a fresh
commitment to obedience. Their obedience, regardless of
circumstance, was the primary concern of God. This theme
permeates all of Scripture: "To obey is better than sacrifice"
(1 Samuel 15:22); "Whoever has my commands and obeys
them, he is the one who loves me" (John 14:21, NIV). So we
must obey what we know of God's Word whether we are
succeeding or failing. Obedience is the way out of failure. It is
the way into success.

Recount how God led you in the past. The past does not
ensure the future, but the past prepares us for the future.
Most of us live in the existential now, somewhat like Christ's
disciples in Mark 6:52: "They had not gained any insight
from the incident of the loaves, but their heart was hard-
ened." God intends for us to recount His past blessings and
lessons as preparation for the future.

We readily admit the value of obedience and remembering, but we resist the *process* of learning the lessons. In

Deuteronomy 8:2, Moses reveals that the purpose of the failure experience was to "humble you and to test you in order to know what was in your heart, whether or not you would keep [God's] commands." All are character development processes.

Testing assesses the strength and value of an object. Without testing we cannot really know the depth of our commitment to God. Testing produces deeper qualities of character and godliness. No testing is too great since we have this promise: "No temptation [testing] has seized you except what is common to man. And God is faithful; he will not let you be tempted beyond what you can bear. But when you are tempted, he will also provide a way out so that you can stand up under it" (1 Corinthians 10:13, NIV). Temptation and testing are closely related. In Matthew 4, we see that Christ was tested and tempted. In most cases they are synonymous. Testing, properly responded to, develops character. Testing, improperly responded to, leads to bitterness and resentment.

"Pride goes before destruction, and a haughty spirit before stumbling. It is better to be of a humble spirit with the lowly, than to divide the spoil with the proud" (Proverbs 16:18-19). Humility is one of life's greatest virtues and is repeatedly commended by God. Pride, its opposite, falls under God's severest condemnation.

Thus, God uses the circumstances of life, like failure, to develop humility as the focus of our character. Scripture reveals what God expects of every Christian: "He has showed you, O man, what is good. And what does the LORD require of you? To act justly and to love mercy and to *walk humbly* with your God" (Micah 6:8, NIV).

Nothing seems to humble us quite so much as failure. And it can sometimes be the experience that turns our life in the right direction. As a young Air Force officer, I entered pilot training thinking that only as a pilot could I advance.

My mind was filled with the glamor of flying. Suddenly, after having done well in nine months of training, I failed a check ride in jet formation flying. Within days I was put out of the program. I was humiliated. But it was a spiritual turning point in my life. It forced me to turn to God for my life's direction and made me stop taking things into my own hands.

In retrospect it was a minor failure. But no failure seems minor at the moment. But God's perspective remains the same. True success is built on the cornerstone of humility, and it may take failure to humble us and to develop our character.

God can also use success to develop our humility, if we view success properly. Often our success is due so little to what *we* have done that we are humbled to realize how God works on our behalf. But learning humility through success is far more difficult for us, since pride comes easily when we are riding a wave of success.

The final part of God's training process reveals what is really on our hearts. Again, the focus is on the inner man, the character. The external evidence of this inner character is obedience to God's Word.

As Moses explained to Israel, the desired result of God's testing and humbling is that we *understand* our total dependence on God's Word. Life is more than "bread"—food, possessions, position, power, even success. Life bears meaning only in obeying God's Word. So again we focus on obedience.

If you are experiencing success right now, remember that God has provided it, not you. Remember also that earthly success is fleeting. Success is not our right, but only a privilege from God for a given time. This could make us fear losing it, but if our focus and dependence are on God such fear is unfounded.

SOME PRACTICAL SUGGESTIONS

What should be my response when I fail—or when I succeed? Certainly God wants us to respond in a spiritual way, even when we are engulfed in the emotions of the moment.

Handling failure. In counseling many people who have been fired or released from a job, we have seen a variety of responses. One extreme is a feeling of worthlessness and failure. The other is a "head-in-the-sand" approach, not acknowledging the failure, but rationalizing and explaining it away. Both are unhelpful and lead to further failures.

In failure we suggest this sequence of responses, as hard as some of them might be:

1. *Thank God.* In times like these 1 Thessalonians 5:18, "In everything give thanks," takes on real meaning. God always means it for good on our behalf, and for His ultimate glory.

2. *Evaluate.* What really happened? We need to know the truth, regardless of how much it hurts. Often, employers or supervisors do not tell the person the real reasons for his or her dismissal. The fact is that most employees do not want to know the truth. They would rather believe their viewpoint of the events. This leaves great room for self-deception. You will have to press people for the truth. When you have the truth, then divide the evaluation into categories of what you can change (work habits, learned skills, etc.) and what you cannot change (gifts, abilities, budget cutbacks, etc.). If you fail to evaluate well, you will lose. In discussions, one response we have heard is, "I want to concentrate on the future, not on the past." Certainly the future is key, but it is vitally important to learn from the past and not repeat the same mistakes.

3. *Be faithful to the basics of the Christian life.* Intensify your time with God. It is vital to know His direction for the

future and to be in tune with Him.

4. *Guard against bitterness.* In all likelihood you have been mishandled or misjudged in some way. That is part of life—injustice. Yet you cannot change that by being bitter. Bitterness and anger only hurt you and those close to you (Hebrews 12:15).

5. *Be willing to wait.* Patience to discover God's plan is key. It also takes time to recover from the emotional blow of failure (James 5:7-8). This can be a time of reassessment. Clearly, if you have no job, waiting may not be an option. Your waiting will be patience in allowing God to work out the details of your life.

6. *Make corrections.* As you assess the lessons you learned from this experience, make sure you respond. Change wrong attitudes, alter your career goals, learn new skills, deal with spiritual issues, learn to develop discipline.

7. *Be aggressive and diligent in your next steps.* Don't quit. Keep your focus on what God has for you. Work harder to learn and develop as you seek out new opportunities.

Handling Success

It would seem that success is easier to handle than failure. In some ways, it is easier for the short term. But success is fraught with many more subtle dangers. Diligence to respond properly is of vital importance.

1. *Acknowledge the source of success—God.* First Corinthians 9:7 teaches that we are responsible for nothing in our successes and abilities. Our talents, heritage, and opportunities are all engineered by God. Acknowledge this in the depths of your inner person.

2. *Be thankful and give God the glory.* Both publicly and privately, give thanks and turn the glory to God.

3. *Keep faithful in the basics of the Christian life.* In success, it is easy to become complacent. The Scriptures and life regale

us with stories of men and women who turned away from God at times of great achievement and success. Keep your spiritual discipline with great care.

4. *Guard against pride.* Success can be the breeding ground for ego and pride. True inner acknowledgment of our debt to God and dependence on Him is the best preventative. One clue of pride is the tendency to look down upon others or to count others as less than yourself in what they have done or accomplished (Philippians 2:3-4).

5. *Use your success as a platform for witness.* Your success is never for your glory. It is always for God and His Kingdom. We must never violate that purpose. In success, look at every turn for the opportunity to give honor to God and share the gospel with others in natural terms (not in odd, overt ways that are stilted). Make yourself available to God in your success.

NOTES: 1. Bob Greene, "Fired Executive Lands on His Feet, But Still Feels Pain, Fear," *The Seattle Times* (August 15, 1979), page 38.
2. A.W. Tozer, *The Best of A.W. Tozer*, ed. Warren W. Wiersbe (Grand Rapids: Baker Book House, 1979), pages 46-47.

Chapter Ten

REAL SOLUTIONS

The Volkswagen "beetle" of the 1960s had no fuel gauge. One drove until the gas tank was emptied and then reached under the dashboard to flip a switch to the "reserve" tank of about one gallon of gas. The great surprise would be to turn on the reserve and find nothing there.

In the stress-filled life of modern man, we live with a similar problem: no ready gauge to tell us when we run out of energy. It seems we are bent on wrecking ourselves on the shores of life with little regard for our limits. Our bodies and minds suffer silently for years only to finally protest in a cataclysm of events that can sideline us for years of recovery.

God never intended that we live hectic, uncontrolled lives. In this chapter, we wish to share some basic principles that can prevent the frantic, compulsive style of living at work, at play, or at home. We call it "building life reserves."

BUILDING LIFE RESERVES

It is not unusual to press ourself beyond our normal limits in many areas of life. For instance, most people can get by on only a few hours of sleep for two or three days, if they are well rested at the beginning. However, if they are already tired, two or three days of little sleep would be almost unbearable and could make them ill.

A friend once shared a helpful illustration on building life reserves. This is a modified version of the illustration.

We all have three major areas of life—physical, emotional, and spiritual. In each of these areas we build up reserves for times of unusual need. Consider first the physical. Imagine your physical being as a bucket (see Figure 10-1 below).

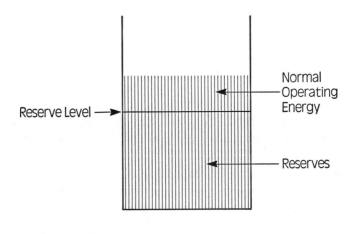

Figure 10-1

When we live from day to day, we burn our physical energy down to the reserve level. Then we replenish it with food, rest, and exercise. Occasionally we dip into the reserves and use more energy than we do normally. It then takes time to replenish our energy reserve.

If, over a long period of time, even our reserve level becomes depleted, we live on a thin edge of existence. (See Figure 10-2 below.) Consider the area of sleep. When you are healthy, a short night of sleep is made up in a day or two. When reserves are low, a short night may require a week to recover, for now there is little or no reserve of physical energy to call upon. The outcome is physical exhaustion or illness, which necessitates a longer rebuilding process.

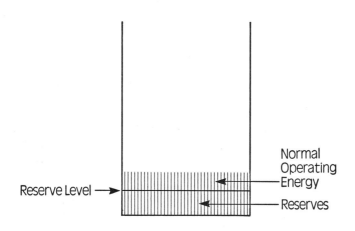

Figure 10-2

Now picture all three areas as in Figure 10-3 on page 180. These three areas comprise our total self. We can operate in several ways:

▶ Above the reserve level in all areas
▶ Above the reserve level in one area and below in the others, as shown

▶Below the reserve level in all areas
▶And a variety of additional combinations

In each area we can dip below the normal reserve level. When a reserve is exhausted, or low, we experience illness (physical), sin (spiritual), or nervous breakdown (emotional).

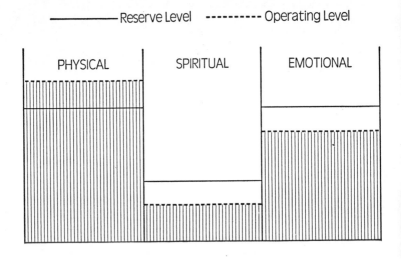

Figure 10-3

This is still not an accurate picture of a Christian's life, for God is the source of supply in every area in our life—the physical and emotional as well as the spiritual: God "has granted to us everything pertaining to *life* and godliness" (2 Peter 1:3); "My God will meet *all* your needs" (Philippians 4:19, NIV); "Seek first His kingdom and His righteousness; and *all* these things shall be added to you" (Matthew 6:33). Therefore, a more accurate picture of life would be as shown in Figure 10-4.

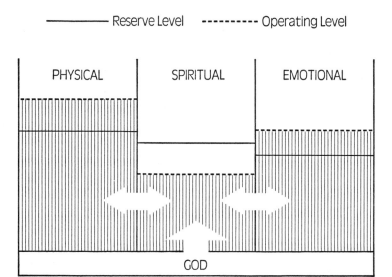

Figure 10-4

Think of the reserve areas as savings accounts. They can either be exhausted or drawn upon in times of need. The three areas exhibit a certain independence and interdependence. *The spiritual area feeds the other two in a primary way.* Of course, our physical and emotional reserves also affect our spiritual intake. Exhausting resources in any area will cripple the Christian's effectiveness.

Compare Figures 10-3 and 10-4. They are different, depicting different people or different times in life. For instance, in Figure 10-4 the person is in good physical health (perhaps a jogger), operating with plenty of stamina. But the spiritual area is low, operating in the reserves (he may be jogging in the morning and spending no time with God). He is doing well emotionally. Think about what the description of the person depicted in Figure 10-3 might be.

Now try drawing a picture of the reserve and operating levels in your life as you see it today.

The next three sections of this chapter give some practical suggestions on building our physical, emotional, and spiritual reserves.

Building Spiritual Reserves

Spiritual reserves provide the foundation for both the physical and emotional areas. They are interdependent, but for the Christian, spiritual reserves give the strength that nonChristians cannot tap.

The primary foundation is Jesus Christ: "For no man can lay a foundation other than the one which is laid, which is Jesus Christ" (1 Corinthians 3:11). Being religious is not sufficient. The only sure foundation is knowing Christ as our personal Savior, experiencing a spiritual rebirth followed by a living relationship with Christ.

"But let each man be careful how he builds upon [the foundation]" (1 Corinthians 3:10). Watch how a master craftsman carefully prepares his materials. He knows which tools to employ. Then he builds carefully, taking time and exercising patience, until he finishes.

Some years ago, Roger Brandt, a close friend and fellow faculty member of the United States Air Force Academy, helped me build some bookshelves. I thought we would slap them together in an evening or two. After all, I had sketched out the plans so all we had to do was build them.

Roger carefully selected and measured the boards. After several checks, he finally cut them to length while I tried to be useful by holding the ends or catching scraps.

Now, I thought, we'll quickly nail them together and be done. But first he grooved the boards to insert the shelves and dividers. Then he used the router to round the edges. Then he rechecked each measurement. Several times he carefully put everything together and then took it apart again to make small adjustments.

The shelves were finally glued (not nailed) and set up. Now to throw on some stain and finish it, I thought. But it was not quite that simple. Roger patiently finished the shelving into a quality piece of furniture. It took almost two weeks, but the shelves still stand in my office after being installed in three homes, and they reflect the quality of the craftsmanship that built them.

I was impatient. I wanted the bookshelves to progress from an idea to reality with little or no effort. Similarly, in the Christian life we want to grow fast. But building spiritual reserves and growing in Christ take time and perseverance. If you build shabbily, your life almost certainly will collapse when you reach a major crisis.

Many Christians go through years of Christian activity reaping spiritual truth vicariously through others. But they have not built their own personal lives on the Scriptures. In times of stress, borrowed truth is like beautifully displayed imitation food behind glass—beautiful to look at, pleasant to remember, but inaccessible and useless. In the midst of stress we are frequently unwilling to build and rebuild our foundations.

Following are three indispensable tools for building the Christian life:

A *daily time of Bible reading and prayer*. This is the simplest, most necessary activity to keep me going as a Christian. A daily time of personal devotions need not be lengthy or complicated—just regular.

The first element of the "quiet time" is Scripture. Begin in the New Testament and read small portions, such as a few verses or a chapter. As you read, think carefully about it and pray about how it applies to your life.[1]

Then spend a few minutes in prayer. Thank God for

what He has done for you. Share your burdens with Him. Pray for your family, friends, and relatives. Many people find it helpful to keep a list of personal needs and prayer requests from others to help them pray more effectively and to record God's answers.

Regularity makes the quiet time with God a strengthening and stabilizing influence in your life. As little as fifteen minutes each day amounts to seventy-five hours a year (over nine full work days!) if you do it only 300 days in that year.

Can you imagine the effect this private time with God could have on your life and outlook? This time must be a priority or it slips away. It is helpful to take time to read the Scriptures *before* doing anything else. Once you have started the habit, you will look forward to it daily as a special time. A realistic goal might be to meet with God on five out of six days a week, one of which should be on the weekend when you can make it a more leisurely time.

Personal Bible study. "For many years Monterey, a California coast town, was a pelican's paradise. As the fishermen cleaned their fish they flung the offal to the pelicans. The birds grew fat, lazy, and contented. Eventually, however, the offal was utilized commercially and there were no snacks for the pelicans.

"When the change came the pelicans made no effort to fish for themselves. They waited around, grew gaunt and thin. Many starved to death. They had forgotten how to fish for themselves. The problem was solved by importing pelicans from the south, birds accustomed to foraging for themselves. They were placed among their starving cousins, and the newcomers immediately started catching fish. Before long the hungry pelicans followed suit and the famine was ended."[2]

This describes many of us. We become so used to letting others feed us spiritually that we forget how to forage in God's Word on our own for ourselves.

The word "study" frightens many of us. We do not think of ourselves as students. Yet, we study all the time. We study how to do a particular task at work. We buy books on auto repair, stereo systems, new appliances, hobbies, sports, and a host of other subjects, to learn how to do something.

When we know what the Bible teaches, we build a key reserve for coping with crises. Secondhand knowledge of the Bible leaves us feeling empty and undernourished. "Be diligent to present yourself approved to God as a workman who does not need to be ashamed, handling accurately the word of truth" (2 Timothy 2:15).

You may feel that reading the Bible is hard enough without studying it too. But Bible study is really quite simple. Here are some easy suggestions:

▶ Use a personal study guide (such as the *Design for Discipleship* Bible study series available from The Navigators), or studies on particular books of the Bible (*LifeChange* series) which can be found in any Christian bookstore.

▶ Meet with a small group. Bible study is difficult (though not impossible) to do alone. We need the stimulation of a small group where we are accountable to prepare and share regularly.

▶ Prepare ahead of time. You will receive in proportion to what you put into the study.

Sermons and Sunday school classes, though excellent input, rarely meet the need for concentrated Bible study, because hearing is the only sense used. Study involves input through your eyes, into your mind, and onto paper.

To find a quality Bible study group, check with someone in your church or ask a more mature Christian to start one. Perhaps you could start one yourself.[3]

Fellowship. "Misery loves company" is an old saying. In the midst of any crisis, we need empathy and help. Mutual sharing and help is what Christian fellowship is all about: "Two are better than one because they have a good return for their labor. For if either of them falls, the one will lift up his companion. But woe to the one who falls when there is not another to lift him up" (Ecclesiastes 4:9-10); "And let us consider how to stimulate one another to love and good deeds, not forsaking our own assembling together, as is the habit of some, but encouraging one another; and all the more, as you see the day drawing near" (Hebrews 10:24-25).

When a crisis hits, our first move may be toward isolation. We are embarrassed and confused, so we withdraw. But we desperately need fellowship and friendship at such a time. You may argue that church services with everyone dressed neatly, singing, listening, and reciting in unison are a far cry from fellowship. But you can meet other Christians there and find out about small groups where *personal* fellowship thrives. If you already fellowship with other believers, don't quit when a crisis comes, for that's when you need it most.

Building Physical Reserves

"Everyone who competes in the games goes into strict training. . . . I beat my body and make it my slave" (1 Corinthians 9:25,27, NIV). God expects us to be good stewards of all He has given us, including our body. No one needs to begin jogging six miles a day or to become a health food fanatic. We simply need to use common sense and a moderate amount of self-discipline.

Eating habits. Americans (including Christians) consume far more food than a population twice our number needs. Yet, we are not necessarily in good physical health.

Overeating, junk foods, and unbalanced diets characterize the habits of many people.

For weight control, push-aways from the table provide the simplest answer, but require much self-discipline. If you learn and practice sensible nutrition, you will feel much better physically.

Physical exercise. Shortness of breath, tiredness, and back trouble are only a few of the symptoms of inadequate physical exercise. Even one who looks trim may simply have a high metabolism and stay thinner without being physically fit. Regular physical exercise will not only make you feel better and possibly lengthen your life, but it can give you a new view of yourself and a new outlook on life.

Until age forty, Mary had no regular exercise. She is not athletic, so only participated reluctantly in sports. Then she began to jog. It literally changed her outlook on life. She developed greater stamina, a more competitive spirit, and a larger emotional capacity. She continues jogging to this day.

Walking, jogging, racquetball, handball, tennis, swimming, and basic calisthenics are all possibilities. If you have any question about your ability to exercise strenuously, be sure to consult your physician. Start slowly, but above all, start and keep it up long enough to enjoy the benefits.

Physical examinations. A friend of ours on Navigator staff, Cecil Davidson, entered his sixties actively leading a ministry to servicemen, even playing football and soccer with them. After some prodding he had a physical check-up and emerged with a bill of perfect health. But how you feel can deceive you. Everyone needs a periodic check-up. Your life may depend on it. Physical problems detected early can often be treated, whereas later, after the illness has progressed, a cure may be hopeless. We suggest a physical once a year, or at least once every two years, after age thirty-five. A medical examination may be expensive, but it is money well spent. It's your life, which is infinitely priceless.

Rest. Regular, effective rest and sleep undergird our entire physical and emotional well-being. Try to determine the right amount of sleep for you and discipline yourself to get it.

Most people require between six and nine hours of sleep. Regularity is as important as the amount. As one becomes older, controlled rest becomes more important because burning the candle at both ends is a sure way of igniting a mid-life crisis. Dr. Archibald Hart observes that most people need more sleep than they think. He does not see any health virtue in sleeping as little as possible.[4]

Building Emotional Reserves

A physical exam tells you the condition of your body. But where do we get an emotional examination? Usually we don't even consider our emotional needs until we approach a nervous breakdown. Emotional evaluations do exist in very limited form and accuracy. They are only indicators at best. One that is readily available is the Taylor-Johnson Temperament Analysis Test. Many pastors and counselors are trained to administer and interpret it. We encourage you to use it to gain some insight into yourself. We took it and found it was very useful.

Emotional repairs are time-consuming and stressful. It is much better to build deep emotional reserves rather than to repair and rebuild. Here we will identify a few key areas that can either build or deplete our emotional resources.

The marriage relationship. One of life's most rewarding relationships takes place in marriage. When that relationship is good, it gives emotional support and replenishment beyond description. When it is bad, it saps every ounce of the emotional reserve we possess. We must exert extra care in building the marriage relationship.

Job and career. Marriage and career fight for dominance in the lives of most men, and an increasing number of women. A positive view of work and career gives great emotional stability. Many emotional resources are expended needlessly at work over matters of very little importance.

Children. In the early years of marriage, children drain us physically. In later years they drain or build us emotionally.

Recreation. In times of stress, diversions and recreation rebuild our emotional resources. Many Christians are so busy with jobs, families, and church that they neglect refreshing recreation. Many families choose recreation that conflicts with church activities or that is more work than rest, which drains, instead of building. We need regular recreational activities interspersed among stressful activities. Some ideas are:

▶ Reading
▶ Hobbies in the home
▶ Sports
▶ Music
▶ Taking a college course
▶ Watching a *specific* weekly television show
▶ Knitting
▶ Photography
▶ Hiking
▶ Gardening
▶ Crafts

Recreation need not be expensive. It need only be different from your required tasks—something you select that brings you pleasure. Its purpose is to recreate your emotions. But recreation does not just happen; it needs to be planned. It will take time, but it is time well spent and will pay dividends for years to come.

Specific emotional drains. Many incidents and circumstances drain us emotionally and create special problems such as:

▶ Unresolved conflicts
▶ Suspicion of others' motives
▶ Overscheduling and overactivity

Each of us can list our own problems almost without thinking. We need to reduce them or learn to handle them better.

The key areas could go beyond the five we have mentioned. Our emotional reserves must be built and protected. They are not manufactured automatically. Many other things can help build this reserve bank, such as:

▶ A strong spiritual walk
▶ Confidence that God is in charge of your life
▶ Rest and exercise; physical and emotional health are closely linked
▶ A good self-image
▶ A few deep personal relationships

KEY BIBLICAL CONCEPTS

The incidents that produce life crises are not the roots of those crises. Their basic cause is an inadequate understanding of God's character and purposes. The primary cures are found by developing one's understanding of God and basing one's life on a strong relationship with Him.

Certain key biblical concepts and doctrines underlie the teaching of this book and the proper response to a crisis. Without Bible-based concepts, we tend to wallow about in the morass of our feelings and emotions, never planting our feet on solid ground. Most of these concepts concern our view of God and how He acts in the world. They are theological issues of deep and far-reaching importance. These issues answer the questions:

▶ Is God still in charge?
▶ What have I done wrong?
▶ What is God doing to me?
▶ Is it too late to get right with God?

One who can respond properly to these four questions possesses the doctrinal foundation to survive any crisis or transition.

The Sovereignty of God (Is God still in charge?)

For centuries theologians have studied, discussed, and written about the nature of God's sovereignty. No one has yet produced an answer that the human mind can easily grasp. The study becomes more complex as we try to explain man's free will versus God's sovereignty. Those concepts seem inextricably locked in opposition to one another. Yet, the fact of God's sovereignty is fundamental to all of life.

Webster defines sovereignty as "supreme power . . . freedom from external control . . . controlling influence."[5] Applied to God, this means He has total authority, power, and control over all creation. God is sovereign in all aspects of our personal lives and in world events. Consider the following statements from Scripture as a summary of His sovereignty.

God is sovereign over nature. "For every beast of the forest is Mine, the cattle on a thousand hills. I know every bird of the mountains, and everything that moves in the field is Mine. If I were hungry, I would not tell you; for the world is Mine, and all it contains" (Psalm 50:10-12). "The heavens are Thine, the earth also is Thine; the world and all it contains, Thou hast founded them" (Psalm 89:11).

God is sovereign over rulers and governments. "O LORD, the God of our fathers, art Thou not the God in the heavens? And art Thou not ruler over all the kingdoms of the nations? Power and might are in Thy hand so that no one can stand against Thee" (2 Chronicles 20:6). "No one from the east or the west or from the desert can exalt a man. But it is God who judges: He brings one down, he exalts another" (Psalm 75:6-7, NIV). "The king's heart is like channels of water in the hand of the LORD; He turns it wherever He wishes" (Proverbs 21:1).

God is sovereign over my personal circumstances. "And we know that in all things God works for the good of those who love him, who have been called according to his purpose" (Romans 8:28, NIV).

God is sovereign over my physical and emotional makeup.

> For you created my inmost being; you knit me together in my mother's womb. I praise you because I am fearfully and wonderfully made; your works are wonderful, I know that full well. My frame was not hidden from you when I was made in the secret place. When I was woven together in the depths of the earth, your eyes saw my unformed body. All the days ordained for me were written in your book before one of them came to be. (Psalm 139:13-16, NIV)

But, if God is sovereign, can I make any free choices? Yes. God has all the powers of sovereign control, but yet allows us to make various choices. He knows what we will choose, and allows us to live with the results of our choices. Yet He specifies certain limits or boundaries. He promises to control the external circumstances of our life for our good. We may not always view our circumstances favorably but He knows what will be for our perfect good. We then select our responses to the external circumstances that God allows.

Perhaps you feel that the truth of God's sovereignty and our ability to choose are diametrically opposed to each other. Yet, both are taught in Scripture. We accept them as facts of Scripture that the limited human mind cannot fully grasp. "'For My thoughts are not your thoughts, neither are your ways My ways,' declares the LORD. 'For as the heavens are mightier than the earth, so are My ways higher than your ways, and My thoughts than your thoughts'" (Isaiah 55:8-9).

For example, the concept of gravity undergirds all space flight and all of human life on this planet. Yet, no one can explain gravity. No one understands where it comes from or what causes it. Yet, we describe it in equations, experience it, and are totally dependent on it for the sustenance of life. Not understanding gravity does not prevent us from recognizing it, living with it, and using it. Similarly, while we may not fully understand God's sovereignty, we can accept it and order our lives by it.

In addition to recognizing God's sovereignty, we must recognize that He *always* has our best interests at heart. "What then shall we say to these things? If God is for us, who is against us?" (Romans 8:31). "Are not two sparrows sold for a cent? And yet not one of them will fall to the ground apart from your Father. But the very hairs of your head are all numbered. Therefore do not fear; you are of more value than many sparrows" (Matthew 10:29-31).

The combination of God's sovereignty and God's love provides a sturdy foundation for living in any circumstance. However, you can choose not to believe these truths. What are the practical results of *not* accepting God's sovereignty and love?

▶ *Fear* that God is not in control and cannot or will not protect and help you.

▶ *Rebellion*, thinking that God is not in control so you can oppose and overrule His ultimate purposes for your life.

▶ *Bitterness* against God for His seeming inability to protect you and control your circumstances.

▶ *Fighting* God for control of your circumstances, assuming that you can escape or control them.

▶ *Uncertainty* about God's purpose or seeming capriciousness in the daily affairs of your life.

▶ *Doubting* God's concern and love for you.

Any one of these attitudes leads to spiritual dryness and a questioning of God's love, motives, and wisdom. On the other hand, accepting God's sovereignty and love for us results in a completely different outlook on life:

▶ *Peace*, knowing that God is in control and guarding your best interest.

▶ *Rest*, knowing you do not need to struggle against God or your circumstances to survive.

▶ *Confidence* in God's power to work on your behalf.

▶ *Faith* in God that grows through the process of seeing God develop the circumstances in your life for your ultimate good.

▶ *Optimism*, knowing that the final outcome and victory are assured.

God remains sovereign whether we believe it or not. The truth of God's sovereignty can be stated briefly and simply, but is so deep and far-reaching that you may want to study this doctrine in much greater depth.[6]

Acceptance of God's sovereignty provides the proper

perspective with which we should approach any problem or crisis situation. In light of His sovereignty we understand several things:

1. God made you with a physical makeup that experiences constant change, development, and decay. A normal part of being human is experiencing the physical realignment of one's body throughout a lifetime.

2. God made you an emotional being with certain personality characteristics, strengths, and weaknesses. The very emotional responses and reactions of life provide the basis for God to intervene in your life in a new and fresh way.

3. Even when many incidents of your past resulted from sin and bad choices, God will now use these lessons to rebuild and mature you from now on. The history of your marriage or singleness, career, and personal accomplishments are under God's sovereign control and will fit His purposes for your future.

4. Whatever your current emotional struggles or problems, God will take you through them and make you into a more mature and happier person. There is *always* light at the end of the tunnel.

5. In the context of God's sovereignty, you still retain the right of choice, but you must live with the results. "Do not be deceived, God is not mocked; for whatever a man sows, this he will also reap" (Galatians 6:7). God *knows* what we will choose. God *could* ordain or determine what we choose, but He does not do so. "He who has My commandments and keeps them, he it is who loves Me; and he who loves Me shall be loved by My Father, and I will love him, and will disclose Myself to him" (John 14:21).

Grace Versus Works (What have I done wrong?)

Any time we face problems we suspect that we have sinned and God is punishing us. Upon investigation we usually find many areas of our lives that God could justly condemn. Then we begin a process of self-condemnation and an attempt at self-reformation. But such a process, though perhaps needed, strikes at the wrong source.

Our past is unchangeable, and an analysis of past sin can preoccupy our minds. We begin doubting the reality of our relationship with God. God fades in our troubled minds as a viable resource and help. We think He is punishing us instead of helping us.

An understanding of grace and works can be a key factor in reversing the downward spiral. It is relatively easy to believe that we are saved by grace. Our relationship with God is based upon grace and finds expression in the teaching of justification.

> He saved us, not because of righteous things we had done, but because of his mercy. He saved us through the washing of rebirth and renewal by the Holy Spirit, whom he poured out on us generously through Jesus Christ our Savior, so that, having been justified by his grace, we might become heirs having the hope of eternal life. (Titus 3:5-7, NIV)

After salvation most of us tend to build our relationship with God on what we do, such as attend church, share our faith, study the Bible, or help the poor. We labor diligently. We struggle against sin. We try to change our habits. We even study key doctrines of justification, salvation, and sanctification. We become doers to such an extent that our relationship with God settles into a series of disciplines, activities, and works. They are good and give great personal satisfaction. We *feel* we are doing something *for* God. But we subtly transfer from dependence on God to dependence on our works and suddenly find ourselves devoid of grace.

Then if a life crisis descends, we experience a mixed onslaught of feelings; the works no longer satisfy because we have a renewed desire to do something lasting with our lives—something more than occasional good works. We feel guilt and a lack of spiritual motivation creeps in. It is precisely at this time that we must return to the basics of our relationship with God. We were saved by grace through faith. "For by grace you have been saved through faith; and that not of yourselves, it is the gift of God; not as a result of works, that no one should boast" (Ephesians 2:8-9).

We cannot work our way into salvation. Nor can we work ourselves out of a spiritual slump.

> As you therefore have received Christ Jesus the Lord, so walk in Him, having been firmly rooted and now being built up in Him and established in your faith, just as you were instructed, and overflowing with gratitude. See to it that no one takes you captive through philosophy and empty deception, according to the tradition of men, according to the elementary principles of the world, rather than according to Christ. For in Him all the fulness of Deity dwells in bodily form, and in Him you have been made complete, and He is the head over all rule and authority. (Colossians 2:6-10)

We are to walk or live the Christian life in the same way that we received Jesus Christ. How was that? By grace through faith. Look at this passage carefully. We have already been rooted in the past, and God did the planting. The word *firmly* speaks of the security and completeness of the roots or planting. The other side of the coin is that we are *now* being built up by God. Verse 10 teaches that we are totally complete in Christ—lacking nothing.

In a crisis we must remember the basics of our relationship with God. No matter how we feel, we are still His children and He has not abandoned us. We only deepen our feelings of anxiety and inadequacy when we desperately grasp at works and activities to try to secure our standing with God. A return to a position of total dependence on Him is necessary to reinstall our confidence and sense of security.

Spiritual Maturity (What is God doing to me?)

Blaming God for our problems and afflictions is as old as sin itself. After all, isn't God sovereign? Couldn't He have prevented this? He must be out to get me. When such thoughts flash through our minds, we almost believe them because of their frequent recurrence.

God's purposes are far deeper than giving out petty punishments for our frequent misdeeds. He wants solid maturity in the life of a believer. The immature bristle with doubt in affliction, while the mature grow and deepen. A foundation of spiritual maturity carries us through *any* crisis.

But what is spiritual maturity? As we examine key passages of Scripture several characteristics stand out.

The spiritually mature person is:

Teachable. He is willing to learn, no matter what the cost. Teachability and humility are twins in practice. "A wise man will hear and increase in learning, and a man of understanding will acquire wise counsel" (Proverbs 1:5). See Proverbs 9:8-10 also. In a crisis the mature Christian becomes a learner, one who seeks and listens to wise counsel.

Sound in doctrine and deep in God's Word. "Since an overseer is entrusted with God's work, he must be blameless. . . . He must hold firmly to the trustworthy message as it has been taught, so that he can encourage others by sound doctrine and refute those who oppose it" (Titus 1:7-9, NIV).

A person who knows the Scriptures and who practices them has roots that will hold fast in any storm. Their soundness and depth are not theoretical, but practical. Such a person does not possess mere head knowledge, but life knowledge. His doctrine and knowledge were formed in the forge fires of life. A mature Christian prepares for crisis by developing depth in the Scriptures. Crises and strong feelings will still come but *there will be roots* when you need them.

Patient—exhibiting self-control. "The overseer must be . . . self-controlled" (Titus 1:7-8). Impulsiveness and anger in a crisis pave the way to defeat. On the other hand, self-control and patience force your mind and actions back to God and the Bible, which give victory. "Yet those who wait for the LORD will gain new strength; they will mount up with wings like eagles, they will run and not get tired, they will walk and not become weary" (Isaiah 40:31).

A man or woman of faith. "And without faith it is impossible to please Him, for he who comes to God must believe that He is, and that He is a rewarder of those who seek Him" (Hebrews 11:6). "Now faith is being sure of what we hope for and certain of what we do not see" (Hebrews 11:1, NIV). The mature Christian possesses tested faith. It is faith experienced in answered prayer, patiently waiting for God to work, obeying God's will, and seeing God's promises fulfilled.

Sensible. "The overseer must be . . . hospitable, loving what is good, sensible" (Titus 1:7-8). Sensible means having good sense or using your head. God gave us a mind and wants us to use it under the direction of the Holy Spirit within the boundaries of Scripture. Clear thinking can rescue us from panic in the midst of a crisis. Impulsiveness and confused thinking will make us more unstable. We need to develop the habit of clear, Spirit-led thinking.

Intent on pleasing God, not men. Habitually measuring our actions by others' opinions and expectations weakens our ability to clearly discern God's will. Remember, we serve God alone (Colossians 3:23-24), but we often guide our life by man's opinions. Man-pleasing is an ulcer-producing activity. Men are changeable, but God is not. He is constant. A mature Christian focuses on pleasing God, not men.

Pursuing a holy life. "But like the Holy One who called you, be holy yourselves also in all your behavior" (1 Peter 1:15). Holiness and Christlikeness are nearly the same. We need to be growing more and more into conformity with Jesus Christ in our thoughts, desires, and actions. Pursuing purity of life and holiness is no small thing. It is a lifelong goal. The constant pursuit of holiness and Christlikeness is a mark of a mature Christian.[7]

Honest. "Since an overseer is entrusted with God's work, he must be blameless" (Titus 1:7, NIV). An honest person possesses a reputation that no amount of power or position can buy. In a world where situation ethics rule everyday conduct, honesty is a rare commodity. Above all, it should be an obvious mark of a Christian. In the midst of a crisis, honesty with yourself and others as to what you are encountering will open new vistas of communication and help.[8]

Unselfish. "Do nothing from selfishness or empty conceit" (Philippians 2:3). Be "free from the love of money" (1 Timothy 3:3). Selfishness and materialism join hands to produce evidence of spiritual immaturity. The Bible says much on the topic of money and possessions, and our attitudes toward them. The mature Christian trusts God for his needs and selflessly gives himself to others without asking, "How much will this cost me?" A focus on obtaining "things" blunts the inner desire to know God and serve others. Christ set the perfect example by giving Himself fully and unselfishly on the cross for our sin to obtain our salvation. One may have been a Christian for many years and still be living selfishly with a materialistic outlook that tarnishes and hinders spiritual maturity. Learn to live for others, focusing on the eternal values they represent.

Steadfast in hard times. "Therefore, my beloved brethren, be steadfast, immovable, always abounding in the work of the Lord, knowing that your toil is not in vain in the Lord" (1 Corinthians 15:58). "In this you greatly rejoice, even though now for a little while, if necessary, you have been distressed by various trials, that the proof of your faith, being more precious than gold which is perishable, even though tested by fire, may be found to result in praise and glory and honor at the revelation of Jesus Christ" (1 Peter 1:6-7). A man or woman who endures difficult times should grow in maturity and dependence on God. Deep roots do not develop in an easy chair during a soft life. They develop through trials and tests that drive us to depend on God.

Forgiveness and Restoration (Is it too late to get right with God?)

Many of us do not turn to God until we despair of any other help. Though it is unfortunate to wait, God still takes us in.

> "Come to Me, all who are weary and heaven-laden, and I will give you rest. Take My yoke upon you, and learn from Me, for I am gentle and humble in heart; and you shall find rest for your souls. For My yoke is easy, and My load is light." (Matthew 11:28-30)

No matter what you have done or are doing, forgiveness is at hand. Simply pray and confess your sin to God. He will restore you to fellowship and begin the process of building or rebuilding right now.

REBUILDING

The bottom may have just fallen out of your life and left you at a low ebb. Perhaps for the first time in your life you see no way out. You have nowhere to turn but to God.

Now God can take over and begin a rebuilding process. It is likely that much of your past life was built around your accomplishments and attempts to be happy and successful. But that is past. Now God has His chance, if you will give Him the opportunity.

How can you rebuild? A few simple ideas follow:

Review your spiritual foundation. Analyze your personal commitment to God. Give thanks for your salvation. If you discover you never really believed in Christ for salvation, do that now. In any event, recommit your life to God and ask for His help today in rebuilding your life.

Admit your present need to God and others. Honestly tell God how you feel and think. Find a Christian friend or counselor who will interact with you as you work through the issues. Don't expect anyone to be an answer-man with all the solutions. God wants to teach *you* and help *you* understand and grow through your circumstances.

Be willing to start over. To rebuild means to start over in many areas: your marriage, your spiritual life, your career, your self-esteem, your physical condition. Go back to the basics and build up some spiritual, physical, and emotional reserves, as outlined earlier in this chapter. Reanchor those moorings one at a time, remembering that it will take patience.

Set goals. Insecurity and anxiety result naturally from wandering blindly with no certain destination. This is the time to set and clarify goals for your life. Begin with small goals to meet immediate needs. Then set goals for deeper and more far-reaching development.

And, whatever you do, don't quit! There are answers. This time will pass and you will either have developed spiritually or openly abandoned a walk with God. You must choose what happens. God is sufficient for your need now. He only wants you to turn to Him in full dependence.

NOTES: 1. Many people use a devotional guide, such as *Our Daily Bread* (available from Radio Bible Class, Box 22, Grand Rapids, MI 49555, free of charge); or *Streams in the Desert*, by Mrs. Charles E. Cowman (Grand Rapids, Mich.: Zondervan Publishing House, 1968).

2. *Bits & Pieces* (Fairfield, N.J.: Economics Press, June 1976), page 23.

3. *How to Lead Small Group Bible Studies*, (Colorado Springs, Colo.: NavPress, 1975).

4. Archibald Hart, *Adrenaline and Stress* (Waco, Tex.: Word, Inc., 1986).

5. *Webster's New Collegiate Dictionary* (Springfield, Mass.: G. & C. Merriam Co., 1973), page 1112.

6. Several excellent books for further study are available: J.I. Packer, *Knowing God* (Downers Grove, Ill.: InterVarsity Press, 1973); J.I. Packer, *Evangelism and the Sovereignty of God* (Downers Grove, Ill.: InterVarsity Press, n.d.); C.H. Spurgeon, *Spurgeon on the Attributes of God* (Tyndale Bible Society, P. O. Box 6006, MacDill AFB, FL 44608); Edith Schaeffer, *Affliction* (Old Tappan, N. J.: Fleming H. Revell Co., 1975).

7. See Jerry Bridges, *The Pursuit of Holiness* (Colorado Springs, Colo.: NavPress, 1978).

8. See Jerry White, *Honesty, Morality, and Conscience* (Colorado Springs, Colo.: NavPress, 1978).

Chapter Eleven

PULLING UP ROOTS

The drive home from work that night seemed to take hours instead of thirty minutes. Phil's heart was pounding, and he felt as if someone had just punched him in the stomach. He was laid off. He had thought his job was totally secure. He knew he was one of the most competent men in his job. But so were a thousand other men who were also laid off that day.

Then began months of searching for work. When the first shock was over, he settled down to a serious search for work in the same city. Soon his determination turned to panic. Nothing was available. He began looking in other locations. Then he heard that he could have a job in a city one thousand miles away. He should have been happy, but he had to decide whether he was willing to pull up roots and move his family. He had lived there fifteen years. He thought of his children—their friends, school, and church. The adjustments could be especially hard for his teenagers.

We live in a mobile society. It has been said that families in metropolitan areas move an average of every four or five years; few children go to school in the same city from kindergarten through high school graduation. The process of moving often causes the children to suffer.

FACTORS TO CONSIDER IN CHANGE

What factors should you consider in making a move or in changing jobs? We will mention only four, though many others could be included. Each is dealt with more fully later in this chapter.

Family

Without question, children suffer the most from a move. They lose their friends, teachers, familiar surroundings, and key extracurricular activities. Adults frequently underestimate the emotional impact a major change has on a child. The older the child, the more difficult the adjustment to new surroundings, for he makes new friends less easily. Months pass before he is thoroughly integrated into a new church or school situation. Children do not direct our lives, but they deserve *consideration* in any decision.

Who *really* bears the major work in a move? The wives. Yes, husbands may do some packing and help load and unload the goods. But who cleans the house to sell, does most of the packing, disengages the children from school, unpacks, lives (and even cooks) out of suitcases in the temporary apartment, cleans the new house, and all the while cares for the children and their needs? The wives. Husbands finish their job, load and unload the furniture, help find the house, and then immerse themselves in the new job. This may not be all bad, but we must face the facts and understand their implications.

A number of years ago my wife had a baby, typed my master's thesis, and made two major moves—all in six months. At the same time I undertook significant ministry that included activities with students in our home. Neither of us realized the physical impact on Mary until almost a year later. Then, for almost a year, we had to reduce our activities until her full strength returned. We learned a valuable lesson.

Church and Spiritual Involvement

Life is a spiritual involvement: everyone receives and gives. You must ask, "Why did God put me here in the first place? Is this mission accomplished?" Vital spiritual nourishment provides the foundation for your spiritual growth. You need the church. You need the fellowship of the Body of Christ. If you and your family are receiving deep spiritual feeding where you are now, you will want to consider carefully before leaving it. If you leave, what spiritual environment exists where you are going? Have you investigated it? How mature are you—can you survive spiritually where there may be little spiritual fellowship?

Besides taking in spiritual food, you also should be giving spiritually to others. What is your ministry now, and what opportunities exist in the new location? By the term *ministry* I mean not just organization functions like teaching Sunday school or serving on a church board, but also outreach to people in the job and neighborhood. Unless you have trained another Christian to replace you where you are, there will be no one to carry on your work.

Your Job

Are you realistic about the demands of your new job? Will it meet your expectations? Will it consume your time? Depending on why you changed or moved, your new job may cause more problems than it solves. Motives—both good and bad—for changing jobs will be discussed in the next two sections.

God's Will
Ultimately you must ascertain God's will for you. No set of rules or guidelines will ever "tell" you what to do. When all the counsel and tests are in, you must find yourself on your knees seeking that final word from God. God longs for the best for you, so take the time and effort to discern His will—and then do it. A brief summary of this subject is provided later in this chapter.

VALID REASONS FOR CHANGE

God directed Moses to leave Egypt for the desert, to return to Egypt, and finally to lead the nation of Israel out of Egypt to the Promised Land. God led David through adversity to live in many places, from caves to palaces. God led Paul on his missionary journeys. Moves and change are not negative; God continually directs us to various places of ministry and work. But when there is a choice, we must consider our real motives for change—and there are good ones. Some we choose, and some God forces on us.

Family
Again? Yes, the family again—first. A friend of mine took a high-paying, prestigious job in another part of the country. He and his wife agreed on a two-year testing period because they had some reservations on the advisability of the move for the family. Neither his wife nor his children ever adjusted to the new environment and relationships. They were not sullen and complaining, but that settled peace was missing. After two years they moved back to their original location with no real guarantee of a job. He did find a job, and the family's contentment was restored.

On the other hand, a time may come when teenage associations need to be severed. Al and Ginger had two teenagers and one preteen. Their city was becoming a center of drugs and student unrest. Though Christians, their two teenagers began to develop relationships and undergo pressures that were deeply affecting their thinking, attitudes, and actions. Although Al's job was rewarding with promised advancement, he decided to move to another city to change his children's environment.

Pay careful attention to your family's needs. You cannot rebuild past years in their lives. There are a number of family reasons that enter into a decision to move:

▶ Health problems of one family member;
▶ Schooling for the children;
▶ A frantic family activity cycle that cannot easily be changed in your current location;
▶ Company pressures and demands that are hurtful to the family.

Your Company Moves You
If you work for a large company that has several locations, the possibility of a move always exists. The company might ask you to move, or economic conditions may reduce work at one plant and confront you with the choice of moving or quitting. You don't *have* to move, yet the economics of the situation may force you to move. It could be a big step of faith to stay and trust God for another job. If you choose to stay, you would want to know clearly that it was God's will, since employment opportunities elsewhere are often uncertain. When you have a choice, seek God's will with your family in your current circumstances.

Personal Satisfaction and a New Job
The challenge and excitement of a new job motivates many people. A new job can offer the way out of difficult working

conditions or an unstable financial situation.

Marty had worked on construction jobs since he was eighteen. The work was seasonal, financially unstable, and left him dissatisfied. At age twenty-three he decided to begin training for other work. For six years, the family scrimped and restricted its schedule so that he could attend school at night. He finally graduated, but there were no job opportunities in his city. After twenty-nine years in one place, three children with deep ties in school and the neighborhood, and a good church situation, a major move appeared to be the only way to break into the new field. After much prayer, Marty and his wife decided that God wanted them to move. The major issues in their decision centered around Marty's personal satisfaction in the job and security for the family. They were not running from anything; he had been well-respected in the construction business.

As Christians we don't operate on the myth that "what is hard is good" or "the opposite of what I want is what God wants." God wants to give us the desires of our hearts and to give us peace and contentment. If we attempt to work in fields in which we lack ability or gifts, personal dissatisfaction soon surfaces. Dissatisfaction often provides a clue that a change could be needed, *provided* our relationship with God is secure and we are not seeking escape from problems.

A new job in a new location can stimulate new ministry opportunities, new contact for witness, new growth by stepping out in faith, and renewed motivation in the job. God opens as well as closes doors. The open door may require a new job and a move.

Changing jobs without changing location can provide new job opportunities or satisfaction without a major disruption of family and church circumstances. Make that possibility a first consideration when you contemplate a change of jobs.

Health

When one member of the family has a significant health problem, you have a clear responsibility to do whatever is necessary to help. A change of climate may be recommended by a doctor for asthma, hay fever, or other illnesses. In many places, expert medical facilities for particular problems are not available within reasonable distances. Sometimes a particular job can cause specific health problems. Mary's parents moved from the Midwest to the state of Washington due to her mother's health. It was a difficult, distressing move for the children. It did not solve the health problem, but it brought Mary to Seattle where we met. We view it as part of God's divine plan.

Remember that many health problems have an emotional base. Such difficulties are every bit as real as a broken leg or a case of flu. Although I hesitate to recommend a change of job or location *only* because of emotional health, we should recognize that location, financial circumstances, the type of job, and church relationships *do* have a profound effect on our emotional health. A different location or job can be restorative *if* the roots of the problem have also been treated.

Opportunities for Ministry

As a person matures in his Christian life, he begins to develop a new view of his spiritual needs, gifts, and contributions. Economic achievement and worldly success lose their glitter. Reality shatters unfulfilled dreams.

An old man brought a painting to a famous painter who asked, "Who painted this?"

The old man replied, "A twelve-year-old boy."

Excitedly the famous painter said, "Bring him to me, and I'll make him the greatest artist the world has ever known."

"That's impossible," said the old man. "I'm the boy."

Life is more than work and money. God plans that you make a particular spiritual contribution, but you need to prepare and train for it. However, opportunity for training can be lost. You must be in the right place. Would you be willing to move in order to get help in your personal life so that you can effectively minister to others? Are you willing to invest time now to be ready for your contribution to the Body of Christ later, not in full-time Christian work, but rather as an effective layman in a secular job? If you find a church or a person who can help you prepare to make an effective *contribution*, seize that opportunity.

A physician friend of ours was offered a prestigious teaching and research position. As he and his wife prayed, they were led to turn it down to focus on opportunities for spiritual growth and ministry where they were living. He was able to cut his practice to four days a week and make more time available for helping people in their spiritual lives.

God can also lead you to move or to change jobs to involve yourself in a particular ministry or outreach. As a young Air Force officer, I was assigned to an exciting job at Cape Canaveral. Through a series of circumstances, God brought the Air Force Academy to my attention. I began to consider the opportunities to witness and minister to students there. Ministry to cadets by outside groups was discouraged, so an inside influence was needed. I began to pray and prepare. I received counsel that the academy was not the best assignment for my career, but I sensed God's leading. After three years of preparation, God led me to a position on the faculty. As a result, several hundred cadets have come to know Christ there and are now vibrant Christian Air Force officers.

Has God been speaking to you about a particular place of ministry?

A New Start

We read frequently of people who make drastic changes in their careers: the engineer who becomes a farmer; the carpenter who goes to college and becomes a doctor; the independent businessman who gets fed up with the pressure and takes a job with hourly pay. Many people do not make the right career choices at first. Should they just accept it as "fate" and "gut" it out for life? Not necessarily. God can lead such a person to a new life and career.

If you became a Christian as an adult or have recently gained new maturity in your Christian life, you may be in circumstances that are too complicated and difficult to restore to bring fulfillment. You may need to make a new start by moving or changing jobs. Allow God to change you and your situation if that is the case.

Laid Off

This chapter so far has dealt chiefly with reasons for job changes within our control. But what about when we have been laid off or fired?

Whenever the national economy changes and possibly deteriorates, increasing numbers of people may be out of work. The illustration that opens this chapter points out the dilemma many face in such a circumstance.

A friend of ours, an engineer, was suddenly laid off. He had thought his job secure, so the layoff was completely unexpected. He anticipated no problem in getting another job but soon found that nothing was available anywhere in the country. Finally, as a step of faith and after much prayer, he and his family sold their house and took their savings, and he went back to graduate school to qualify for work in a different field. During the months of job-hunting, the family was quickly enlightened about the status of the unemployed. Even in their church relationships, people rarely offered help or inquired about their needs.

Writing on this subject in *Eternity* magazine, Sara Welles said, "Our friends at church either smiled weakly or avoided us. I remarked to my husband that it was almost as though one of us had died. People acted afraid or embarrassed."[1]

Being without work is frightening and unnerving. It hurts our pride and drives us to God. It certainly provides a legitimate reason for a move. But what do you do when you lose your job? Here are some practical suggestions:

1. As hard as it may be, thank God for your circumstances.
2. With your wife or husband, list some lessons God may want you to learn in this circumstance.
3. Take a financial inventory: What are your savings? How much unemployment compensation can you draw, and for how long? What insurance policies do you have with cash value for a loan? What do you have that can be quickly converted to cash if necessary—e.g., a second car or a recreational vehicle? Avoid borrowing money at interest.
4. From this financial inventory, determine how long you can be without work and still subsist.
5. Work out a severely reduced budget. Cut all frills. You can probably live on one-half or two-thirds of your previous income. Do *not* use credit cards. If you have heavy debts with high time payments, write to your creditor explaining your situation and try to make a reduced payment.
6. Discuss your situation with your family. Pray together. This will rally the family together and will help them be willing to live on less.
7. Let your pastor know your circumstances, and ask the church to pray. Tell your friends; they may

know of other employment.

8. Don't be too proud to accept food gifts or other offers of help. Allow others to have the joy of sharing, but don't expect it as your "right."

9. Inform your out-of-town friends and relatives that you are seeking a job. They may know of opportunities.

10. Immediately begin to seek work. If a résumé of experience would be helpful, begin writing one. The local library has books to help you. If you are a poor writer or organizer, ask your spouse or a friend to assist you.

11. Apply for unemployment benefits. You and your company have paid for these benefits: they are not a handout. (This statement has been challenged in several seminars. Someone always pays the bill— usually your previous employer.)

12. Plan to put in eight-hour days in job-hunting. That is your "job" now. Send your résumé to out-of-town employers early, since it will take time for them to reply.

13. Always seek a personal interview with the one responsible for the hiring.

14. In the process of job-hunting, you will usually find some inadequate, low-paying jobs not in your field. Keep a list of these jobs. You may need to take such a job temporarily. In fact, if this kind of job is available at night or part-time, take it. You can continue to hunt for a better job during the day.

15. Consult an employment service, making sure it is reputable.

16. Consider the possibility of retraining or schooling. This may be your opportunity to change fields.

17. If as a husband you are out of work and your wife

does not work outside the home, you may want to consider the possibility of your wife working, at least temporarily.

18. If work is not available locally, think seriously of changing locations.

19. Above all, improve your personal walk with God. He may be trying to get your attention.

We also recommend reading the book *What Color Is Your Parachute?—A Practical Manual for Job Hunters and Career Changers*, by Richard Nelson Bolles.[2]

"You Are Fired."

The words "You're fired!" bring chills. When it happens, it seldom seems justified to the employee. But it does happen. Whether the reasons are valid or not, the fact remains. You are without work, and the record of being fired is in your employment history.

It may be helpful to know some of the major reasons people are fired:

▶ Poor work performance (quality, speed, or production),
▶ Job beyond a person's ability or training (unqualified),
▶ Bad relationships with others (conflicts),
▶ Making serious errors on the job,
▶ Laziness or intentionally slow work,
▶ Undependability.

When you are fired, you can follow essentially the same suggestions given in the previous section. However, first a warning. You may have been "fired" even though the terminology used was "laid off." Usually you know when that is the case. If this was your situation, you must admit it or else you will not learn the lesson God has for you in the experience—and you will repeat the mistake in your next job.

Now follow the guidelines stated in the previous section. Remember that no failure is final. Good performance on the next job will erase the stigma of being fired.

QUESTIONABLE REASONS FOR CHANGE

Just as there are valid reasons for changing a job or location, there are also questionable reasons for changing. Several of these reasons, mentioned earlier, bear repeating in this context.

Money. Money could be a reason for a change, but seldom should be *the* reason. If you live at or below the subsistence level, a change for more money is valid. If you change just to get more money for more material things, that is questionable.

Career climbing. Be cautious about changing jobs or locations to advance in your career. This reason must coincide with careful considerations of the family's needs and other factors. One or two changes for career purposes could be acceptable, but frequent moves when your children are older can create problems. When the children are young, moves are less traumatic for the family.

Running from problems. Look closely at the problems you are experiencing. If they are primarily of your own making, changing your job or location will not solve them. Running away is not the answer. Do everything you possibly can to solve them without a move.

The company says so. This by itself is not sufficient reason to move. It is only a factor. You can quit or take a lower-paying job in the company.

TOO LATE TO CHANGE

Is it ever too late to change job, career, or location? Ideally, we would like to say "never!" Realistically, limitations do exist. The three factors that must be considered are

▶ time and age,
▶ finances,
▶ family.

If you are in your late forties or older, age limits the feasibility of a new job or career. Many companies hesitate to hire people in that age bracket unless they have unusual qualifications or experience (e.g., an expert machinist or an executive). The ideal time for a new career change is in the thirties. Then you know many of your own abilities and limitations and still have extensive time to be productive for a company in your new career. Time is a factor in retraining and preparation for a new job. Some careers require several years of training, and others take only months.

The greatest barrier to career change is lack of finances. Most people simply do not have the money to tide them over a period of education or training. Many do not have enough to make a move for a new job. But if God's will is clear and your desire is great, it can be done. If you qualify as a veteran, don't forget the GI bill as a source of financial aid for education and formal training. Student loans with low interest and liberal repayment terms are often available. Much training and education can be obtained in night courses. You and your spouse may need to work part-time for a couple of years. Without question, sacrifice will be involved. But sacrifice now is an investment for the future.

If you are contemplating a job change (not career change), begin a savings program and tighten the budget now. Often you must take a pay reduction to begin work in a different locale or company. But take warning not to be a job-hopper: employers are suspicious of frequent moves.

Since sacrifice of some kind often accompanies job and career changes, you must ascertain the total impact on your family. Is it fair to them? Do they support the change? Will it rob your children of their most valuable possession—you? Can your husband or wife undergo the pressures resulting from your decision? Do not sacrifice your family for your personal gain or satisfaction. But take into account the possible future benefits the change may hold for them.

It is never too late to change, but the cost increases with time and age. You cannot always wait for things to be better—they probably won't be.

GUIDELINES FOR FINDING GOD'S WILL

Everyone wants a magic formula for finding God's will. We want one-two-three, no-fail instructions with a money-back guarantee. But there is no such thing. Walking by faith is the heart of the Christian life. And to walk by faith we must know God's will in small and large things. Yet knowing God's will and doing God's will are not the same. Knowing but not doing is sin; doing without knowing is folly.

God wants us to know His will: "So then do not be foolish, but understand what the will of the Lord is" (Ephesians 5:17). God promised us guidance: "I will instruct you and teach you in the way which you should go; I will counsel you with My eye upon you. Do not be as the horse or as the mule which have no understanding, whose trappings include bit and bridle to hold them in check" (Psalm 32:8-9). Although an automatic formula does not exist, there are well-known and tried principles that will guide you in finding God's will.

A Personal Walk with God

Unless you are in a right relationship with God, trying to find His will in some major or minor decision is presumptuous. God has more basic things to communicate to you. If you are having difficulty determining His will, examine these prerequisites:

1. Are you a Christian? God responds only to His children. If you have never personally asked Jesus Christ to be your Savior, you cannot expect guidance from God.

2. Have you confessed known sin? There may be factors in your life that God has been showing you for some time. "If I regard wickedness [sin] in my heart, the Lord will not hear" (Psalm 66:18). To clear the lines of communication, confess your sin to God (see 1 John 1:9).

3. Are you in daily fellowship with God through Scripture reading and prayer? Would you go for days without listening or speaking to your spouse? Similarly, God wants us to have daily communication with Him.

4. Are you obeying what you know? We are already aware of many things God wants us to do. These include:

   ▶ vital fellowship with other believers in a church,
   ▶ an open identification with Christ by your action and verbal witness,
   ▶ a scriptural family relationship.

God may have shown you His will in the past and you refused to obey. Until you do what you already know of His will, you cannot expect guidance. The story of the nation of Israel in the Old Testament proves that they *knew* God's commands, *refused* to do them, and were *separated* from God's continued blessing—*until* they repented and began to obey. (See Nehemiah 8 and 9 for an excellent summary on this point.)

Pray

The next step is to pray. Quiet your thoughts and ask God to make you willing to do whatever He directs. Pray regularly about the details of your decisions, and ask for His guidance. Pray with your family and ask others to pray (Matthew 7:7-8, 1 Peter 3:12).

Use the Scriptures

As you read the Word regularly, ask God to impress on you statements or ideas that shed light on your motives, thinking, or decisions. Do not expect to be "told" by a Bible verse what you should do, nor turn automatically to passages that favor your desire. Simply ask God to use His Word and His Spirit to speak to you. Avoid jerking verses out of context and making them say things God never intended. Look for direct commands and principles (see Hebrews 4:10).

Examine Circumstances

Get the facts. Write them down. At this point write down as much as you can from facts, Scripture, and counsel. Words on paper are often more objective than feelings and impressions.

Obtain Godly Counsel

Others can often see things we cannot. They ask questions that cause us to consider new directions. They may discern faulty thinking or even sin. Counsel only with Christians when spiritual matters are involved. "How blessed is the man who does not walk in the counsel of the wicked" (Psalm 1:1).

There are times, however, when it is proper to counsel with nonChristians. For example, in gathering data on a particular job, factual information about a city, or advice on your qualifications for a position, it would be in order to heed counsel of nonChristians. But when the spiritual dimension is needed nonChristians can offer nothing. Be careful not to "stack" your counsel by going only to those you know will give a decision for you—and you must not expect anyone to do so. On highly emotional issues such as marriage, there is a tendency to seek counsel from various persons until you find someone who agrees with your desire and opinions. Carefully guard against that possibility (see Proverbs 15:22).

Personal Desire

Your personal desires are important. God wants you to have joy. If you are in fellowship with Him, your personal feelings and desires can be an indication of God's direction. Write down your personal inclination. On paper it may prove obviously emotional or strongly of the flesh. Written desires also help you to relate your personal feelings to the facts and circumstances (see Psalm 37:4).

Patience

We usually try to hurry God. Our byword is "now." God often says "wait." We want God's direction immediately, but growth and maturity are evidenced by willingness to wait on God (see Psalm 37:7, Hebrews 10:36, and James 1:3-4).

Lorne Sanny, former president of The Navigators, once told me, "There are good decisions and fast decisions, but there are no good, fast decisions." Yet there are occasions when time is essential. God is a God of perfect timing; He will give you direction when there is a deadline. But do not be forced into a hurried decision when there is excessive pressure and you do not have God's clear direction. Wait upon God.

Consider your health. *Never* make a decision when you are ill, depressed, or fatigued. Never make a major decision when you are angry or emotionally upset.

Peace in Your Heart

"Let the peace of Christ rule [be the umpire or arbiter] in your hearts" (Colossians 3:15). God gives a settled peace to those who do His will. It may not be the candy-sweet, good-feeling peace you sense when sitting in the sun on your day off. Nor will it be the euphoric excitement you feel after your team has won. You can have peace in the midst of fear—the solid assurance of knowing you are doing God's will.

When I began to consider returning to school for a Ph.D., I fought the idea. I did not want to go. I knew how much work was involved. I knew I risked failure. When I made the decision, I was apprehensive—but I knew it was what God wanted. I knew I was in God's will even in the turmoil of fear. Then I had to deal with the anxiety as a spiritual problem, but I still knew the decision was right.

A warning is in order. If you are not in fellowship with God, Satan can give you a false sense of peace. Therefore, never use peace or any one of these indicators alone as confirmation of God's will. They work together.

Decide and wait. Often it is wise to make your decision and then wait a day or two to let it settle before communicating it to others. If in a day or two you still know it is right, proceed with action. F.B. Meyer says,

> Never act in panic nor allow men to dictate to thee; calm thyself and be still; force thyself into the quiet of thy closet until the pulse beats normally and the scare has ceased to disturb. When thou art most eager to act is the time when thou wilt make the pitiable mistakes. Do not say in thine heart what thou wilt or wilt not do, but wait upon God until He makes known His way. So long as the way is hidden, it is clear that there is not need of action, and that He accounts Himself responsible for all the results of keeping thee where thou art.[3]

Depend on God to supply wisdom. If you are walking with God, He will give you wisdom as you make wise choices with your mind. Guidance is not always phenomenal in nature. Often it is Spirit-led common sense. Use the sanctified judgment God has given you.

Don't turn back. Whenever a right decision is made, Satan will send doubt and uncertainty. What God has shown you in the light, do not doubt in the dark. Beware of turning back when you have clearly found God's will. J. Oswald Sanders says, "Having put your hand to the plow, resolutely refuse to turn back. Otherwise, our Lord says you are 'not fit for the kingdom of God.' Never dig up in unbelief that which was sown in faith."[4]

Now act. Make all these steps in prayer and the Word; give God the chance to speak to you in all points; now act. Act in faith on what God has graciously shown you.

HOW TO PULL UP ROOTS—GENTLY

Digging up a live plant and replanting it so that it lives is a delicate procedure. You begin loosening the plant by turning the shovel in the soil without touching the roots, carefully start to lift it out—ever so gently—keeping as much dirt on the roots and severing as few roots as possible. Then in replanting, you reverse the process, giving the plant extra water, food, and care. We know how to move plants, but do we know how to move people—especially little people—our children? Some roots will be severed, but it can be done without killing their spirits and crushing their happiness.

Here are some key points to consider as you move your family from one place to another. No move is ideal, but some are disasters. Seek the best possible circumstance.

Prepare. The more you prepare for your move, the less turmoil you will experience. Don't leave matters till the last minute. It will drain the entire family physically and emotionally.

Involve the family. Just as you would involve the family in the decision to move, now involve them in the process of moving. Get their opinions on what to move, how it will be done, and who will do it. Try to understand their feelings.

Timing. Whenever possible, move at a convenient time for the children. If they are in school, try to move during the summer, spring, or Christmas break. Also ascertain your spouse's needs in the timing. You may need to consider going to the new location ahead of time by yourself.

Advance arrangements. Try to go to the new location well ahead of time to determine the situation. Where are the good schools? Where are the growing churches? What is the housing market? If necessary, make arrangements for temporary lodging for the family before they arrive. Place more emphasis on the school and church situations than on proximity to your job or style of house. Whenever possible, move directly into your permanent housing.

Take time off. Take adequate time off on both ends of the move in order to give the move your full attention. Don't try to finish your work one day and move the next. If necessary, use accumulated vacation time to do this.

Get settled quickly. The sooner you are settled in your new house, the sooner it will be home to the family. Although you may get physically settled quickly, don't expect miracles in getting a family emotionally settled. It takes time to develop new relationships. After one move our family made, it took almost three years before one of our daughters finally announced, "I like this place better than our last one." Avoid reflecting verbally on the merits of the place you left; if you are content, it will greatly aid the children's adjustments. Find a church home quickly so the family can initiate Christian relationships; try to avoid months of church-hunting. Plan to spend extra time with the family to help them through the move emotionally.

Above all, remember that home is not a house. You make the home. We have moved many times, and it has never brought serious readjustment problems for the children. There were strains and fears, but they were secure with us. God is your security; you are theirs.

HOW TO START A NEW JOB

Your start on a new job is as important as your later performance. Some people get off to a bad start and never recover. First impressions last a long time. Early relationships, good and bad, color your enjoyment of work for years to come. Knowing a few basic principles can avert great emotional trauma.

Concentrate. Plan to give your job 110 percent of your time and energy for the first month or two. That is the reason for getting totally settled first. Gain the family's support that this will be the priority. Learn your new job well.

Know what is expected. What is your job? Precisely what are you expected to do and know? Find out; assume nothing; make notes; do extra study. If you are unsure, ask questions. Ignorance is tolerated when you are new: it is inexcusable later.

Be a learner. Every job has its peculiarities—or at least the people do. Ask questions or directions. It is better to ask than to make a costly mistake. Do not feign ignorance, and don't act as if you know it all, but honestly try to learn.

Develop relationships. Get acquainted with your co-workers. They are generally more approachable when you are new. You can ask them questions and get help. Don't waste company time talking, but take every opportunity to communicate. This will lay the foundation for enjoyable working conditions and for a future witness.

Extra effort. Don't be afraid to put in extra hours and extra effort. Aim for quality performance. In a straight eight-hour factory or shop job, you may not be able to work additional time, but you can study on off hours. Most equipment has some kind of manual: use it. You will not be able to make this extra effort all the time, lest you cheat your family, but it is possible for the first few weeks or months of your job. It will provide good job "insurance."

Be a finisher. Unfinished work helps no one. You cannot sell a half-made product. Therefore develop a reputation for finishing what you start—on time. In earning a reputation for dependability and faithfulness, you reflect the character of God.

NOTES: 1. Sara Welles, "When Your Husband's Out of Work and the Church Just Smiles," in *Eternity* (October 1974).

2. Contact Ten Speed Press, Box 4310, Berkeley, CA 94704; available in paperback. Or check with your local bookstore.

3. F.B. Meyer, source unknown.

4. J. Oswald Sanders, *A Spiritual Clinic* (Chicago: Moody Press, 1958), page 183.

Chapter Twelve

VOCATIONAL CHRISTIAN WORK

Full-time Christian work was a career for which I had no interest or inclination. In my early Christian life I had no leading to it, nor was it attractive to me. Yet, about midnight one night in May 1972, I found myself on my knees telling God that I was available, and that I would resign from my career as an Air Force officer to be on the full-time staff of The Navigators.

Many were critical of my decision. Some were skeptical. One retired officer told me I was "insane." My grandmother cried. My wife was initially apprehensive. Most of my relatives were shocked. Others thought it was a great step of faith. The step seemed illogical, because I had only six and one-half of my twenty years' service left until retirement. Many thought I should wait until then.

What led me to this decision?

I was not dissatisfied with my Air Force career. I was a major and had been given pleasing assignments. I had earned a Ph.D. and was in a good career field. In fact, I thoroughly enjoyed almost every aspect of my job, and the family enjoyed the lifestyle.

It was not that I was ineffective in ministry as a layman. In six years of teaching at the United States Air Force Academy I had been able to develop a significant outreach among the cadets. We saw several hundred young men receive Christ, and many of those became committed disciples who potentially would have a profound effect on the entire Air Force as they entered positions of leadership in the future.

It was not that the "offer" from The Navigators was too good to refuse. In fact, there was no "offer" at all. I would have to raise all of my own support, since The Navigators operate as a faith mission and the position had no guaranteed salary.

My real motivation stemmed from a deepening conviction from God concerning my spiritual gifts and my principle ministry for the future. As I became more involved in a discipling type of ministry as a layman, I found that I would have to limit my activities in either the job or my personal ministry to meet my family's needs adequately. As my children grew older and needed more of my time, my job was also becoming more demanding and time-consuming. Something had to give. At the same time, the results of our spiritual ministries to people clearly indicated gifts and abilities of that kind. I was leaning more and more strongly to people-centered interests rather than science-centered.

A significant factor was my longstanding relationship of almost seventeen years as a layman with The Navigators. I had experienced the results of this ministry in my own life and had reapplied it outward to others. I had already determined that if God did call me to a full-time outreach ministry, I would like to work with The Navigators.

Yet, in the process of making my decision there were no clear indicators. Counsel was divided. Pros and cons were fairly balanced. Certainly there would be no greater reward for vocational Christian work than for my work as a layman. Ultimately it came down to prayer and guidance from the Scriptures in making my final decision. And now, after over fourteen years of ministry with The Navigators, I have absolutely no regrets or second thoughts. In fact, we never experienced any regret. God has clearly led and has given a settled peace.

Through this process—and in my task of counseling many others considering a similar step—I have made several observations and drawn several conclusions about leaving the secular world to enter vocational Christian work. Note that the focus here is not on a student selecting vocational Christian work for his first occupation, though many of these ideas may be helpful in such a case.

DEFINITION OF VOCATIONAL CHRISTIAN WORK

Any discussion of vocational Christian work arouses certain feelings of fear, prejudice, or misconception. Even before attempting to define the terms, note that the expression *full-time Christian work* is not used. The premise of this book is that all secular work is spiritual and every Christian is "full-time." Therefore, the term *vocational* describes a person who has chosen some aspect of work in a church, Christian organization, or mission group as his occupation.

We will define vocational Christian work by two categories of function and two of location. The functions are:

Direct ministry function. This includes all ministry directed toward people—either Christians or nonChristians. It includes pastors; Christian education directors; evangelists; missionaries in church planting; teachers in Christian schools; field staff of outreach organizations like Youth for Christ, Campus Crusade for Christ, and The Navigators; and Bible teaching or exposition. Broadly speaking, this function entails "speaking" gifts (teaching, exhortation, evangelism).

Serving or support function. This includes administrators, mechanics, secretaries, computer programmers, some executives, accountants, printers, builders, and myriad other roles necessary to any organization. This involves "serving" gifts (see 1 Peter 4:11).

The two categories of location are:

Foreign. This is any vocational Christian work conducted while living and ministering in another country and culture. It could include ministering to a distinct subculture in one's home country (such as to the American Indians).

Home. This is ministry in the home country that involves no major travel or cultural adjustment.

The term *missionary* is generally applied to the "foreign" category. I prefer a broader definition that includes a person ministering in a situation other than a local church in his own country (such as a missionary to students).

MYTHS OF VOCATIONAL CHRISTIAN WORK

George dedicated himself to foreign missionary service in the closing meeting of a mission conference in his church. He was twenty-nine, married with two children, and a successful construction foreman. After three years of Bible school he was sent to a South American country to plant churches. Four years later George returned disillusioned, bitter, unsuccessful, and discouraged—a missionary "dropout." Why?

Let us probe George's history a bit. He had never led another person to Christ. He was a mediocre Sunday school teacher. He earned straight Cs in high school Spanish. Bible school was a struggle, but he was encouraged to press on with the explanation that his age made it more difficult. His mission board interviewed him primarily on doctrinal issues, rather than about functions he would be required to perform in his missionary work. When he arrived on the field, George found intense conflict among the senior missionaries and little positive training or supervision. Language study was disastrous. Then he found that although he could organize men to build a building, he could not bind people together around a spiritual objective. In construction work, he knew that if a man could not pound a nail straight after a month of trying, he never would and the best solution was to fire him. So George fired himself from the missionfield and came home.

This illustration could just as well describe a pastor who failed to help a church progress, a youth director who was unable to work with people, or an evangelist who seldom led people to Christ. Missionary dropout rates are very high: twenty-five to fifty percent after the first term. There are multitudes of trained pastors who no longer lead churches.

It is no disgrace to leave vocational Christian work, any more than changing jobs or careers in any other context is a disgrace. Yet, in the eyes of the Christian community, that person is often branded as a failure.

Misconceptions and myths about vocational Christian work persist in the minds of many. Those considering it envision certain advantages and blessings. These are some of the myths:

Christian work is easy. Many people view Christian work as an escape from the secular rat race. However, most vocational Christian workers of my acquaintance put in from fifty to seventy hours a week. The schedule may be flexible, but it is never-ending. Rarely is there a real day off; the worker is always "on call." He is usually a motivated person, aware that he is living on "God's money," so he must produce well.

Seldom is Christian work easy. Even support people sense the call to work harder and longer. No church or organization will employ for long a staff person who shirks his work.

There is less pressure to produce. If anything, there is more pressure to demonstrate success in vocational Christian work. The problem is how to measure the product. But even with that ambiguity, people make evaluations. Some common measurements are number of meetings, attendance at meetings, conversions, baptisms, counseling sessions, and numerical growth in specific kinds of ministry. For support staff, the evaluation is like that in a secular job: work accomplished.

There is a more spiritual environment. This may hold true to a limited extent, but people in vocational Christian work are not automatically any more spiritual than those in secular work. They sin, they make mistakes, and they work in the flesh. At times their situation is more difficult, because in a secular environment there are no spiritual expectations; in Christian work the disappointment runs deep when matters are handled in an unspiritual way. Incompetent managers are as common as in secular organizations.

There is less conflict. Whenever people are involved, there is conflict. Sometimes the conflict escalates higher than in a secular context because spiritual overtones give every issue a second face. Spiritual relationships in Christian work heighten the intensity of conflict. Churches split, pastors are dismissed, church staff cannot get along—all evidence that the threat of conflict is ever present.

But the Bible gives guidelines for resolving conflicts. When these guidelines are followed, a unified work environment is created—one that a secular context can never provide.

There is adequate time for prayer and Bible study. Virtually every person in vocational Christian work has more demands on his time than he can possibly fulfill. He battles to find sufficient time for prayer and Bible study as much as before. When he does study, he may battle guilt feelings for not being out "doing" something.

Entering vocational Christian work requires a sacrifice. Many people suspect that the Christian worker will make great financial sacrifices. Is it a sacrifice to be in God's will? Certainly not: it is a privilege and blessing. Missionary Jim Elliot wrote before his martyrdom,

> He is no fool who gives what he cannot keep,
> To gain what he cannot lose.

Materially, God is the great Provider and meets real needs. Riches rarely come to the Christian worker, but we must not assume that he is to be poverty-stricken as proof of his calling. Some may endure difficult times financially, but many positions in vocational Christian work now provide adequate salaries. The most difficult circumstance may be in "faith" missions that offer no guaranteed salary. More and more churches and organizations are beginning to raise wage scales on the biblical basis that "the laborer is worthy of his wages" (Luke 10:7, 1 Timothy 5:18).

In many overseas mission assignments, there may be sacrifice in terms of health, family circumstances, and personal comfort. We would not minimize this sacrifice, but many missionaries never think in terms of sacrifice because they experience satisfaction in knowing they are where God wants them.

You must have a mysterious "call." Do you need some mysterious or emotional "call from God" to enter Christian work? Although some may claim this experience, it should not be the norm. We cannot support from the Scriptures that such a call is different from a call to serve God in a secular vocation. In either case it requires finding God's will.

For Christian work, God simply begins to move a person in that direction by giving him fruit in a particular ministry and speaking to him through the Scriptures over a period of time. I would never discourage the missionary conference appeal, since God is not limited to one particular method of calling. But do not wait for the "feeling" or "call" before considering vocational Christian work. God may be trying to get your attention in other ways.

God may be speaking to you through the Word daily as you see more clearly the urgency of reaching the world for Christ. You may be seeing fruit in spiritual ministry now, indicating a gift that is greatly needed on the missionfield. Since God is sovereign even in your acquaintances, He may be putting you in touch with people who will urge you to consider vocational Christian work. Allow God to lead quietly through your normal circumstances.

The need constitutes a call. Without question, the demand for men and women in Christian ministries greatly exceeds the supply. Nevertheless, a specific need does not constitute a call. Each person must consider his or her own special gifts and God's personal leading as well as the need. Desperate needs will always exist, but God does not necessarily call a person to fulfill what he observes as a need. God's "needs" *will* be met; man's "needs" will not and should not be met. Emotional appeals for help ring from every quarter, but they are not the call—just opportunities.

My gifts will be used more fully. The Scriptures do not teach that a spiritual gift should be used exclusively in a full-time ministry. There is no indication that they are more adequately or more fully utilized in that circumstance. Your gifts can be fully used in any context. However, each job in vocational work does require specialized types and capacities of gifts, so you may be excluded from certain ministries, or directed toward others, by your gifts and capacities.

THE GREAT NEED

The myths of the preceding section are meant not to discourage, but only to inject realism. People *are* dying without Christ; mission efforts *are* being crippled by the lack of prepared personnel; countries *are* closing to missionaries; churches *are* desperate for qualified staff; mission boards *are* searching for people with special support qualifications. Matthew 9:37-38 will always be true: "Then He said to His disciples, 'The harvest is plentiful, but the workers are few. Therefore beseech the Lord of the harvest to send out workers into His harvest.'"

But the true need can be fulfilled only by *committed, qualified,* and *trained* people. There is no room for incompetence. God's business should be done with excellence. Standards must be high, and the training thorough.

Every Christian should consider the possibility of vocational Christian work. Give God the opportunity to lead. Inquire about opportunities. You may be gifted, but are you available? You may be available, but are you trained? Above all, are you committed to Christ and maturing spiritually?

Paradoxically, I must admit that God has used some very unlikely people in the past—people who, in man's eyes, were not qualified or trained. But they had the lost of the world on their hearts, and they were called by God, as evidenced by the fruit of their lives. Who would have selected the Apostle Peter (a fisherman) or William Carey (a shoemaker) or D.L. Moody (a salesman)? Though we as humans plan, evaluate, organize, and decide, God supercedes such limitations. The man or woman does not exist whom God cannot use.

In today's climate where many countries are closing to normal missionary admission, consider going outside your country in your secular vocation. Businessmen, scientists, engineers, and teachers can often go where no professional missionary can. Perhaps God put you in a particular vocation to prepare a way for you and others to penetrate other countries and cultures with the gospel.

GUIDELINES FOR CONSIDERING VOCATIONAL CHRISTIAN WORK

Most Christians, at some time in their lives, sense an urging or an interest to consider vocational Christian work. After receiving specific leading from God, you must answer this important question: "If I enter a Christian ministry, how can I be certain I will be effective?" Here are some suggested guidelines to help you determine if you should make a move to vocational Christian work.

Scriptural qualifications. The most important guideline is to meet the biblical qualifications for church officers in 1 Timothy 3 and Titus 1. They deal with an individual's spiritual maturity, reputation, family life, and personal walk with God. Though every Christian should seek to meet these standards, they constitute a necessary minimum for anyone considering vocational Christian work or positions of spiritual authority. If this standard is violated, the ministry will be corrupted. Therefore, examine yourself in the light of these requirements.

Discerning your spiritual gifts and abilities. God has endowed every person with particular gifts and abilities. You should be able to evaluate your abilities. If you do not have a reasonable estimate of your own abilities (see Romans 12:3), how can you determine where to make your contribution? How can you know? Only by the fruit of your life.

Look at results, not potential. If you are an evangelist, where are your converts? If you are a teacher, have you had successful teaching experiences? If you are a leader, where are your followers? Your gifts and abilities should match the task to which you are called. A good heart and a willing spirit are not substitutes for God-controlled ability. The former attempts, and the latter accomplishes.

DETERMINING THE EXTENT AND CAPACITY OF SPIRITUAL GIFTS

You need to see the results of your gifts and abilities. But even beyond that, you need to have an idea of the extent of your abilities—in other words, your capacity. Not everyone who has a particular gift can produce the same results; there will be differences in effectiveness. You may be able to lead a small group of people, but not a church of four hundred. You may communicate well to large groups, but cannot teach or train leaders individually. You may have led personal acquaintances to Christ, but cannot evangelize strangers.

Determine not only *what* you can do, but also *how well* you do it. Training will increase your effectiveness, but it will not greatly increase your capacity. A mature person should have a knowledge of his capacity as well as his gifts.

But if you *do* have the right abilities and gifts, you bear a responsibility to God to be available to Him full-time. Don't hide behind false modesty or a weak estimate of yourself. William Carey considered himself to be slow in mind, yet he influenced India for Christ by translating the Scriptures into a monumental number of Indian languages. Determination and diligence will succeed where fleshly ability fails. But think of the impact on the world of demonstrated ability *with* determination and diligence!

Get Evaluation
Always secure objective evaluation from others of what you have done and can do. Be specific. Cut through the niceties

of polite compliments. Your life is at stake, and no amount of kind words can replace truth. You should raise questions, such as:

▶ What are a few of my strengths?
▶ How do you know? Specifically, how have you seen this demonstrated?
▶ What are a few of my weaknesses?
▶ If I were to enter Christian ministry, what would I do well?
▶ What would I have a difficult time doing?
▶ How do you feel I would do at (name the task you are considering)?
▶ What evidence have you actually seen that gives you that impression?

Ask several people who know you well to help in this way. You may even ask nonChristians, such as your employer—not for counsel, but for evaluation. At this point you are gathering information and evaluation, not asking counsel. Concentrate on facts, and write down the key points of each evaluation, then begin correlating them to see if some agreement emerges.

Do not neglect to evaluate yourself. Even with personal emotional involvement, you can be factual and honest about yourself to some extent. And, of course, your spouse should be asked to evaluate you as objectively as possible.

THE CHALLENGE

There is great need and opportunity. If you are qualified and called, vocational Christian work will give you fulfillment far beyond your expectations. But it cannot be used as an escape; you will be the same person with the same spiritual problems. You will encounter the same conflicts and power struggles. As Christians, we are in a battle for the lives of men and women, so opposition from Satan is inevitable wherever we are.

A successful accountant recently asked me about accounting in a Christian organization. He liked his work and was having a ministry with people. But he wanted to see his efforts contribute to an enterprise of lasting value, rather than counting money for people trying to get rich. He subsequently joined the staff of a Christian organization in which he could use his accounting skills.

I have no regrets about my personal decision to enter vocational Christian service. God clearly led, and I am greatly fulfilled. But I do value those thirteen years in a secular job. They were excellent preparation.

When all the facts are in and you know what God wants, you must act. No ledger sheet of pros and cons will act for you. You must step out on *raw* faith. That is real life in a secular job or in vocational Christian work—living totally by faith. There is no substitute. It alone brings fulfillment.

> And the LORD said to Moses, "Is the LORD's power limited? Now you shall see whether My word will come true for you or not." (Numbers 11:23)

THE FINAL ACT—MINISTRY AFTER RETIREMENT

In the past year, I have had several letters from people retiring (early or on time) who want to give themselves to ministry, financing these ventures themselves. What a challenge. Rather than escaping to leisure and fun, they are now refocusing their lives in areas of need in the world of the church, missions, and outreach.

I would encourage every man and woman to consider

this. But in doing so, several cautions are in order.

Your secular experience alone will not qualify you if you have not practiced a consistent spiritual life for several years. You still need to meet spiritual qualifications.

It is unlikely that you will hold positions of responsibility or decision-making regardless of your previous experience. Consider yourself in a period of training for at least a year.

Be realistic as to the extent of your contribution. Many churches and organizations are not geared up to absorb volunteers productively. Also, they often cannot give extensive supervision.

Make sure your values and spiritual outlook are compatible with the place you choose to work.

Consider projects or limited time involvements in order to focus your contribution.

Chapter Thirteen

WORKING WOMEN

IN THE MARKETPLACE

The changes in women's employment patterns over the last quarter of a century impact our entire society. The home, the church, and the marketplace will never be the same. This is an age of incredible adjustment regarding the place and influence of women in our world.

Some question the movement of Christian women into jobs outside their homes. They cite the need for stable family environments and personal parental care for children, confused roles in the home, fewer women available for church ministries, and materialistic motives for work. We would agree that all of these are potential problems. Although all of these objections may be well-founded, the raw facts remain:

▶ Women often marry later today and must support themselves when single.

▶ Christian husbands desert their wives. Subsequently, divorced women must work to support themselves.

▶ Fathers abandon their children and refuse to pay child support, and then mothers must support the

children completely.
▶ Widows find themselves in financial desperation and must work.
▶ Families cannot manage if a husband's salary is meager or even nonexistent for a time.
▶ Few church budgets include significant amounts of money to help divorced and widowed women, or even families where husbands and wives are unable to work.
▶ A women's family is grown and she finds time to work as well as manage a home.
▶ Women want to use their training and talents.

For these reasons, and more, women work. In fact, many *must* work. There is now a small but growing movement of women who look for employment that they can accomplish in their homes—crafts, childcare, computer work for business, specialty food preparation, product sales to name a few. But these opportunities are available to only a limited number. Most women who wish to work, or are compelled to work, must go into the marketplace. Women are becoming more and more of a force in the workplace and in society.

Even as we address the realities and the difficulties facing working mothers, we stress the importance of a woman's influence in her home. When children are in their early formative years, it is wise for a mother to consider working only in an extreme situation. The training and character development of a child are responsibilities given by God to parents, and only in unusual circumstances should they be delegated to others. If a husband and wife together decide that the mother must work, a careful search should be made to provide proper care for the children: not someone who will ''look after'' a child, but a trusted individual who has the same principles and goals and standards as the parents, someone willing to teach and train the child when the parents are absent.

Are there illegitimate, wrong reasons for a woman to work? Yes, and here are a few:

Escape from the home. One married woman said, "I can't stand to be home all day. Housework is so boring, and the kids drive me up the wall. I work just to get out of the house."

More money for luxuries. Another woman said, "My husband has gone as far as he can in his company. He's too old to quit his job and look for other work. I'm working so I can have some of the good things that he can never give our family. I want to move to a better house, and for once, we're going to go someplace exciting for our family vacation."

Status. To many women, status comes with a nice home and material advantages. But real security comes only from God and not from any position of employment. Holding a job to gain status, material advantage, or position will lead to frustration and failure.

Pat worked until shortly before the birth of her first child. Eleven years later, after the youngest of her three children entered school, she returned to a secretarial job. She felt that the "extra money" would be helpful, though her husband received adequate wages. The first few weeks were hectic as Pat learned her work responsibilities and tried to balance her time between her job, her husband, her children, and the housework. She was perpetually fatigued, but felt that once she found the balance between home and work, she would feel better. Months went by and, though she learned the job well, Pat never found time to schedule all the activities she considered essential. She struggled with the situation for a year, finding the job becoming more monotonous, her children more rebellious, and her husband bewildered. Finally she quit, feeling she had been a failure, but unable to continue in the situation.

Ann was twenty-eight, unmarried, an excellent secretary, and frustrated. She had completed a two-year secretarial course with honors and for eight years had worked for the personnel director of a large company. She knew she was efficient and capable, and she had the complete trust of her boss, but she was also aware that she had climbed her career ladder about as far as she could go. She knew the job well, and while it pleased her to do excellent work, few new challenges confronted her. She had a succession of roommates, some she hardly remembered. She attended a church with strong Bible teaching, but few single adults. Most of the singles helped in the children's department of the Sunday school and seldom interacted socially. She felt at peace about the fact that, at least for the present, it was God's will for her to be single; though she dated occasionally, no permanent relationship seemed to develop. If anyone had asked Ann to characterize her life, she probably would have said "lonely."

ADVANTAGES AND BENEFITS OF WORKING

This chapter addresses a few issues of special value to women. These advantages are not comprehensive since all the other chapters apply to women also.

Financial Profit

Without question, most women work to have more money. The need may be crucial as we have already said, in the case of the single woman, the divorcee, or the widow. Or the pay may contribute to providing for needs for the betterment of the family or survival in "hard times." Money as an end in and of itself, or as a means for acquiring more "things," is an improper motive for working. Wages that are helping to fulfill a genuine need are honorable.

Claire exemplifies the woman whose income is essential. She is in her early forties with two children who are approaching college age. Three years ago her husband was seriously injured in an industrial accident. Although he receives some financial compensation, Claire returned to work to bolster the family budget and to secure a college education for their children. The experience unified the family as they discussed and decided together that Claire should find a job and that her husband and children would carry the load of housework.

Claire's situation raises a key point. If a married woman works outside the home, her husband should be willing to shoulder a significant share of the housework. However, most married women in the workplace find they still bear the majority of household chores—a fact which increases their time pressures. When single women share a residence, they should equitably share in the efficient functioning of that household.

Use of Gifts or Natural Talents

A young secretary we know has been married three years, has no children, and finds holding a job a profitable use of her time. She is intelligent, organized, and efficient. She frequently evaluates what is best for her, her relationship with her husband, and her home. To this point, she has continued working.

Many women are suited to particular work and find their abilities used fully in their jobs. Before taking a job, a woman should evaluate her capacity, her interests, and her abilities, then search for the appropriate work. She should also determine if she can handle full-time work or if a part-time job would fit her schedule better. There are many aptitude tests that can give counsel toward a particular field.

Contact with People

Working provides opportunities for association with others that can be socially and intellectually stimulating. There may be opportunities for relationships that will lead to evangelism or helping people to grow to Christian maturity. Working gives a sense of involvement in the real world: but do not rely completely on your coworkers for this involvement. Often employment relationships are temporary and transitory, and lasting relationships may not develop on the job. Satisfying and fruitful friendships should also be formed in your neighborhood and church.

Maximum Use of Time

Working women are forced to structure their schedules and use their time to bring the most benefit to themselves, and to their families if they are married. One young wife told me, "If I didn't have a job, I would sleep until noon and never get anything done. It helps me get going in the morning and organize my time."

PROBLEMS OF WOMEN IN THE MARKETPLACE

Fatigue

Most working women find themselves caught in the crunch between their jobs, their homes, and their personal lives. Christian women want to excel in all areas of life, but often find themselves exhausted and live on the thin edge of chronic fatigue.

A young working woman told us, "Since I instituted a daily and weekly planning time, I usually have *time* to get things done. My problem is that I often lack the energy. If I carry out my planned schedule, many times I end up exhausted."

This problem can be met by incorporating the help of

other family members, cutting back on working hours, lowering housekeeping standards, dropping outside activities, or quitting the job altogether.

Boredom

Despite publicity about joining the work force to find "fulfillment," few truly stimulating and energizing jobs exist, especially in jobs occupied mainly by women. Many jobs are routine to the point of monotony, offering little or no opportunity for creativity or advancement.

One way to battle this disadvantage is to do the best possible work at all times, maintaining a standard of excellence that will provide a measure of challenge. Keep Colossians 3:23 continually in mind, making service to Christ the motive for your work.

More importantly, boredom frequently has its root in doubting and questioning whether we are in God's will. If you are convinced that God has directed you to work and has provided the job, you have a sense of purpose that will do much to eliminate boredom in even the most routine of jobs.

Time Pressures

Christian women want to maintain good family relationships, close friendships, and participate in spiritual activities even when they hold down full-time jobs. They also want to keep high standards in their homes. Pressures inevitably result, such as:

▶ How much time with family members?
▶ How much time for personal interests?
▶ How much time for housekeeping?
▶ How much time at church functions?
▶ How much time for personal devotions?

The list goes on. You must make frequent evaluations and adjust the use of your time accordingly. What are the essential requirements on your time? What can be eliminated? Should something be added that is now missing?

If you are married and have a family, determine the needs of each family member, and how they can be met and the time it will take. Include such things as children's extracurricular activities, recreation and devotions with the family, church commitments, social endeavors, and special family interests—that is, to keep spiritually, mentally, and physically whole. When pressures are heavy, it is easy to neglect the activities that develop us as persons. Carefully guard a time each day for personal fellowship with God—Bible reading and prayer. That crucial time will flavor your relationships for the rest of the day. Include time in the schedule for an activity that is particularly for you—perhaps an exercise group, a painting class, voice lessons, an evening class at a local college, craft sessions, or volunteer hospital work.

Materialistic Outlook
Most people in the working world are motivated by a materialistic approach to life. Guard against this subtle trap. Know the reasons why you want to earn money. Keep a detailed account of your expenditures to discover if the objectives for your wages are being met. Attempt to live modestly rather than extravagantly. Often little extra money remains after all the new expenses are met for clothes, transportation, eating out more frequently, and childcare.

Negative Effect on the Family
There is a danger that a woman's absence from the house during her working hours can have a bad effect on her family life. Husbands may be resentful of her full schedule and

apprehensive about their children's care. The children may feel unrestrained and uncared for and, also, imposed upon if they are required to shoulder more responsibility than they can handle emotionally. It is possible, too, that if a Christian woman cannot handle the two roles well—homemaker and working woman—she may emphasize achievement in the more public aspect of work and neglect the first responsibility God has given her.

Moral Pressures in the Working Environment

A young secretary said, "It's a real struggle to keep my eyes on the Lord Jesus when I'm exposed to the world's thinking and value system. It's a test of faith that I must admit I sometimes fail."

Working daily with nonChristians brings Christians under pressure to succumb to their values and world views. It takes a daily commitment to God and a strong faith to resist the temptation to conform.

Sue married while very young. When her two children were still toddlers, she started to work as a salesclerk in a large store. Her husband was a bus driver. She was intelligent and capable and quickly advanced to buyer and than to department manager; her husband remained in the same job. Sue began to experience a vague embarrassment when introducing him to her new associates. After a few years she developed an interest in another buyer, divorced her husband, and remarried. Sue was a Christian, but allowed the world's thinking patterns to become her own.

The moral pressures of the work environment can discourage or possibly tempt a Christian woman. Crude language, dirty jokes, and sexual innuendoes must be faced by all women. The impact seems especially heavy on a single woman, since many men consider her "fair game." The pressure comes not only from men, but from other women who have succumbed to immoral relationships. The surest protection from such pressures is a consistent walk with God. These guidelines may prove helpful:

▶ Make your stand as a Christian known.

▶ Do not give your approval to improper or immoral actions or statements.

▶ Voice your disapproval of crude language or jokes. You can politely and sincerely say, "Mr. Henry, I'd really appreciate it if you would not swear so much. I know you have the right to do it, but it really makes my job difficult." If you are a hard-working employee, your request will carry some weight.

▶ In some instances you may have to quit your job if the moral situation becomes unbearable.

▶ Dress tastefully, not provocatively. Do not encourage advances in any way. Avoid idle flirtation. It is impossible for moral impurity to result without mutual encouragement.

▶ Remember that no job is worth compromising your convictions.

▶ Committed Christians can change the environment of an office, so be a part of the solution to the moral problem.

▶ Try to develop genuine friendships with nonChristian women through your job. Moral pressure and crude language will come from them, and honest friendship will help influence them and alleviate the problem.

Opportunity

No matter what laws are passed or what court decisions are made, employment opportunities for most women remain unequal. For single women who *must* have employment, this can be distressing. Often pay is not as high for a woman as for a man doing the same job. It is at this point that the Christian woman faces a dilemma, one she may face for life. How she responds will largely determine her response to a multitude of future life problems: if she becomes bitter and resentful, she will carry it into her Christian life and witness; if she responds with hatred and radical political activity, she will be deterred from the goal God has set for her; if she accepts the circumstances and seeks to effect change by competence and Christian witness, she will at least be able to influence the status of others where she works and at the same time clearly share Christ.

Spiritual Dangers

Do you keep spiritually fit in spite of the pressures of your job? Are you careful to recognize sin as it enters your life and to deal with it completely? Evaluate periodically the totality of your life and where your job fits into the objectives God has for you, because there are problems that can creep in.

Complaining. It is common to hear people complain about their jobs, their boss, the company, the conditions, or their coworkers. Much of the grumbling is based on fact—inequities do exist—and it is easy for a Christian to join the steady stream of complaints. Christian women, whether in or out of the home, need to keep Philippians 2:14 always in mind: "Do all things without grumbling or disputing."

Resentment. Unless we accept adverse circumstances as an unavoidable condition of life, resentment will flood in. Some women resent their particular job: the pay is too low, the boss too demanding, the working conditions too difficult. Other women resent having to work at all. Perhaps their husbands are incapable of working or receive wages too low to meet the minimum family requirements. Guard against directing resentment against other people. God has ordered your circumstances; accept them from Him.

Guilt. Many working wives, especially if they have children, simply cannot find the time to accomplish all they feel they should do at work, at home, and with their families. They move through life in a fog of guilt, wishing they could be more or do more. You must recognize your limitations, accept them, and live within them. If God has clearly directed you to take a job, and you and your husband feel confident about that decision, then press ahead in your work and never allow yourself to feel guilt about the things you simply cannot do.

PROBLEMS OF SINGLE WORKING WOMEN

The single working woman faces problems unique to her circumstances. The world of the single working woman differs significantly from the married woman's by the absence of family responsibilities associated with husband or children. Although a single man also encounters crucial problems, he does not face the complexity of opinions and situations that confront single women.

Competition for Careers

Single women must approach their jobs as though they plan to remain for an extended length of time. This means that they want jobs with challenge, opportunities for advancement, and fair salary. In a traditionally male realm, competition is keen for the better positions. It is difficult for many women to summon the aggressiveness needed to meet the struggle for advancement. Not all single women want a competitive environment or advancement, but unless they have some special skill or level of competence, job security is endangered. As a single working woman, you must learn to live confidently in a competitive environment even though you may not be by nature a competitive person.

How should you as a woman respond to the demands and circumstances of competition? The statements on competition in Chapter 7 will be helpful, but these may be added:

▶Resolve before God any bitterness or resentment that may have built up as a result of competition.

▶Determine whether you are a competitive person, and if so, in what ways.

▶Commit your position and your job to God in prayer.

▶If you are not competitive in the sense of trying to gain new responsibilities, then concentrate on proficiency and excellence in your current duties. Compete only against your own standard for yourself. Set your own specific goals for personal improvement and proficiency.

▶If you are a competitive person and wish to gain responsibility or a new position, you must be both proficient where you are and train yourself for increased responsibility. Before you compete, be sure that you have the ability to do the desired job. Only frustration will result if you obtain the goal and cannot produce.

▶Do not compete against your coworkers, but only against your own or the company's standards. Personal competition can be emotionally destructive and disastrous for relationships.

▶You may work in circumstances where there is a strong partiality to men for any promotion. As a Christian, you may need simply to accept this limitation and do the best you can rather than arm yourself for battle to change the system. God is in charge of your life and job (Psalm 72:6-7). However, if you see clear preferential treatment, bring it to the attention of management. Don't always back down when you are wronged.

▶Finally, do not give your life and emotional energy to something that does not ultimately count. Place job and position in the perspective of God's total plan for your life. Reaching people with the gospel is far more important than career advancement.

These guidelines are helpful for all working women, but especially crucial for single women.

The Constant Pressure of Decision Making

As a single woman, you probably have no other person to whom you can consistently turn for help and support when making decisions. In marriage there is (or at least should be) constant dialogue on the full range of problems, but the single woman must make all her own judgments. Yes, there are roommates and friends who can offer counsel, but they bear none of the ultimate consequences of the decisions. Only you can carry that responsibility.

Certainly any woman can develop expert decision-making ability. But many women tire of the constant pressure of that process, especially in terms of finances, automobiles, insurance, home repairs, and myriad other matters historically relegated to men. When pressure and discouragement are at a height, there may be no one around to offer refuge.

Yet God has put you in these circumstances and provides what is needed to live joyfully and contentedly. "Seeing that His divine power has granted to us *everything* pertaining to life and godliness, through the true knowledge of Him who called us by His own glory and excellence" (2 Peter 1:3). God has certainly put you in a place where *He* is your only source of strength and provision—but you must draw upon that source. The ultimate issue is your relationship to God both in salvation and in daily living.

If this pressure concerns you, review the discussion in Chapter 3 and especially consider these factors:

▶ Make sure you are developing a daily devotional life in which your focus is on your relationship to Christ. He is your only source of strength, so do not cut off that source.

▶ Develop a few close friendships with single women who have spiritual depth. Avoid a rapid succession of roommates. Deep relationships are basic to happiness.

▶ Foster good communication with your parents whenever possible. They can give valuable counsel.

▶ Develop friendships with one or two married couples who are genuinely concerned for your welfare. There are many couples who would take an interest in helping in mechanical and financial matters. The friendship should be primarily with the wife to avoid problems of questionable relationships.

▶ Do not be afraid to ask for help and counsel when you have a genuine need. Many do not offer help simply because they are unaware of any need.

▶ Take it upon yourself to learn basic skills of finance and home and car repairs. You probably can do much more in these matters than you think.

The Marriage Issue
Society—and especially Christian society—makes the single man or woman painfully aware of his or her "deficiency" in not being married. Thus, even when the issue of marriage has been prayerfully committed to God, it is constantly surfaced by others.

Few women do not desire marriage, and few are closed to the possibility. Yet there are many godly women whom God has led to be single, at least for the time being. First Corinthians 7 certainly authenticates, and even elevates, the single state. Single women can make a special contribution to the Body of Christ and have an unusual devotion to Him (1 Corinthians 7:32-35). A godly single woman is far better off than an unhappy wife in a desperate marriage. The church has much to learn in this regard.

Yet you must face reality. There are pressures from many directions. There are certainly frequent questions and desires from within a single Christian woman. If you desire marriage, you should not be hesitant to pray about your desire, but that desire must not control you. God has a significant contribution for you to make *now* that cannot be made in marriage. Do not thwart His plans by restless impatience that prevents you from doing God's will now. Commit the timing and possibility of marriage to God: you are His, and He wants the best for you. Then you will need to recommit it each time you sense the marriage issue beginning to control your thoughts and dominate your prayers.

In a society of Christians in which marriage is the norm and singleness is viewed as the exception, it takes a deeply committed woman to remain a victorious Christian rejoicing in her state and calling. God's grace is sufficient (2 Corinthians 9:8).

WORKING WOMEN AT HOME

Recently, we have heard a few voices proclaiming the benefits and privileges of homemaking. Some professionals, secular as well as Christian, have willingly withdrawn from their careers to devote all of their time and energies to caring for family and home. During the past two decades, women who worked only in the home were often subjected to insulting and degrading comments about "housewives," and the fresh trend away from this is welcome. As we have said, work in the marketplace is a must for some, but when women have options, the call to remain at home appeals to many (Titus 2:4-5). Working at home offers many benefits, as well as problems.

When our friend Beverly graduated from business college at age twenty-one, she obtained a well-paying, stimulating position in a growing company. She worked for two years, then married an engineer she met in the career group at her church. In the first two years of their marriage, two baby boys were born. The adjustments Beverly needed to make were tremendous. She no longer controlled her own time, finances were tight, she felt pressured by the unending needs of her husband and two sons. She wanted to have a spiritual influence in her neighborhood and church, but could never seem to find the time. She began to resent the demands on her in her home and felt chronically fatigued, often sick.

Homemakers like Beverly number in the thousands—perhaps millions: vaguely dissatisfied, unchallenged, harried, tired. What a distressing waste of potential, energy, and capability!

Many women have been influenced by the recent vehement attacks on the career of homemaking. The inferences are made that the value of work is based on the salary level and therefore, since homemakers receive no salary, the work must have little worth.

Every woman who feels called by God to remain in her home needs to have

▶ biblical conviction for the value of her work,
▶ an efficient plan for maximizing her own potential as a person and as a worker.

Proverbs 31 describes a wife and mother who has the approval of God. She is efficient, industrious, organized, energetic, generous, family oriented, dignified, kind, and spiritually mature. The job of homemaker is not identical with housekeeper, though that is part of the work; perhaps more than any other employment, it is a reflection of the character and personality of a woman. Homemaking is one of the few jobs in which completed results can be observed, both in terms of a house that demonstrates the care and creative capacity of the woman, and people (husband and children) who reflect the daily influence of the wife and mother.

Advantages and Benefits

Independence. A homemaker has considerable freedom to establish and follow her own work patterns. She does not report to an "employer," though there are responsibilities to other members of the family. For the most part, she can set her own work guidelines and standards. She can determine her own priorities and interests and adjust much of her time accordingly.

Creativity. A flexible schedule allows for time to include creative projects. Some are naturally a part of homemaking. Others, while they contribute, are more a personal expression of ability and taste. A few of these creative interests are:

> ▶ being the major influence in children's lives;
> ▶ decorating;
> ▶ crafts (a wide choice);
> ▶ clothing design;
> ▶ creative writing;
> ▶ study of nutrition;
> ▶ gardening (indoors and out);
> ▶ music.

In a real sense, a home is an extension of a woman's personality, where she is free to demonstrate her interests and talents to the fullest extent time will allow.

Schedule flexibility. Few jobs allow the flexibility of homemaking. Although it is essential to efficient homemaking to follow some kind of schedule, that can be arranged according to the requirements of the family and the personal needs and interests of each woman. Often a woman can reduce or increase her workload to suit her standards and activities.

Ministry opportunities. A home is an ideal place to demonstrate the love of Christ. Because she has a relatively flexible schedule, a homemaker can invite others into her home—individuals or groups—for specific spiritual purposes. A home can be used for Bible studies, evangelistic meetings, dinners with nonChristians, and time with needy Christian or nonChristian friends. Some mothers of young children might feel they cannot use their homes for such activities, but if you cannot conveniently host a dinner, put your children to bed and invite someone for a late dessert and coffee afterward. Find a reliable baby-sitter to care for children during a Bible study, and share the expense with the group. Allow God to use you and your home.

Support of husband in family goals. An enriching and satisfying aspect of homemaking is the involvement with a husband and children. Every other job focuses on production, people, or profit unrelated to your personal life. In your home you have the privilege of giving your life and energy to something that is part of you—your husband and your children. To be involved in fulfilling their goals is one of God's highest callings. Although the husband is ultimately responsible for making decisions in the family, the wife sets the atmosphere in the home where those decisions are carried out. Usually she is the parent who has the major day-today influence on the children.

Without this perspective of family support, housework and the other functions of homemaking become empty and purposeless. The objective is not a clean house, but an atmosphere for family growth. The specific activities of a homemaker, though somewhat satisfying in themselves, are most fulfilling as they contribute to building and supporting the family. The biblical principle of giving and then receiving even more in return is nowhere more evident than in a woman's giving to her husband and children.

Problems and Disadvantages for Homemaker

Monotony. Many tasks in the home are routine. Boredom can quickly result if precautions are not taken. The work must be done, but monotony can be reduced by creative planning. Whenever possible, do the routine, least enjoyable chores first in your schedule. If the work does not require mental concentration, use the time to listen to profitable radio programs or tape recordings, to tell Bible stories to your children, and even to talk on the telephone. One of the best investments in our home is a long cord on the telephone receiver so that I can move about as I talk. Keep in mind that monotony is not unique to housekeeping but is a standard aspect of many jobs. The homemaker is fortunate in that she has more flexibility of schedule and more opportunity to inject interest into her job than most other workers.

Confinement. There is an element of what pioneer women used to call "cabin fever" that seems to strike most homebound women now and then. It is the lack of freedom to be out of the home and around other adults consistently. Mothers of small children find this especially true. They develop a conscientious responsibility for their children but feel tied down and isolated.

If a sense of confinement becomes a problem, you can

alleviate it. Invite other women in similar circumstances into your home. Arrange for responsible care for your children while you do something that is personally stimulating for you. Express your frustration to your husband: he just may have helpful ideas. In fact, he may even arrange free time for you by taking care of the children.

Long hours. No other occupation requires an employee to be on call twenty-four hours a day, seven days a week, year after year. For women who do not know how to schedule their work, and who fail to make time for spiritual development and personal interests, the long hours can be devastating. Every homemaker needs to evaluate her workload periodically to eliminate unnecessary tasks, to persuade other family members to share some of the workload, and to make the schedule as efficient as possible.

Self-pity. Many women are prone to the sin of self-pity. They feel that their lives are more difficult than others'. They use their mental energies imaging what their lives could be like, if only . . . .

Women who indulge in self-pity fail to comprehend God's sovereignty in their lives. They don't realize, or don't wish to realize, that God controls all circumstances. Counting blessings is a helpful exercise, but not usually successful unless accompanied by a recognition of the sinfulness of self-pity and a positive determination to eliminate it with God's help. Self-pity and resentment concentrate on wrongs (often imagined or exaggerated). This leads to bitterness and resistance to circumstances. It assumes that God did not know what He was doing when He allowed certain things to happen and prevented others from happening.

Envy. This sin is especially acute when a woman is a "housekeeper" and not a "homemaker." Then the emphasis is on things instead of people. In a materialistic society, a focus on possessions is doubly dangerous for a Christian.

There is a danger for envy to creep in when comparisons are made about personal appearance, capabilities, and gifts.

Every woman must have a clear perspective of who she is, of her gifts and talents, and of her capacities and limitations. Some things can be changed. If you are too heavy, diet. If you are lazy, work. But if you are too tall (in your estimation), accept the fact and have the assurance that God knew what He was doing when He made you. If you have a physical limitation that cannot be changed, accept it and find ways to live fully in spite of it. Comparisons with the circumstances of others always lead to problems. Envy and jealousy are two destructive sins: don't fall into their trap.

Complaining. The aforementioned spiritual dangers can be hidden with no outward evidence. But after they have taken root in the heart and flourished there for a while, they inevitably emerge and are reflected in a barrage of bitter complaints. "Better is a dry morsel and quietness with it than a house full of feasting with strife" (Proverbs 17:1). Do you often feel a complaint straining to be voiced? Learn to direct that complaint quickly to the Lord instead of your family, and ask Him for a thankful spirit.

Materialism. Many Christian women devote their time to selecting, obtaining, and maintaining possessions in their homes. Their security and self-esteem come from a houseful of modern (or antique, as the case may be) furniture and appliances. It is all going to "rust and burn" (Matthew 6:19-21). We need to be very careful that we don't give our lives to things instead of people, that we don't devote our energies to the accumulation of possessions instead of the practice of the Christian life.

Goals. Do you have specified goals for your housekeeping, your personal development, your family? Do you have plans for wisely using your time to meet these goals?

Perhaps you consider yourself a free spirit who works

by mood and inspiration, not by schedule. Strangely enough, the right moods strike too seldom. More often, procrastination becomes a habit, and goals are never met.

Remember that you must be flexible. If your child is ill or needs a listening ear and counsel, that should take precedence over cleaning the bathroom. If a friend experiences a family emergency, delay papering the bedroom walls. Instead, prepare a meal to take to her home. If your husband wants to discuss a job change, by all means delay the dusting.

The needs of people, especially in your own family, always come before the needs of a house. Note the word *needs*. Children occasionally make unreasonable demands; a gentle explanation with an interesting alternative activity can occupy the time of a fretful, obstinate child. At one time I had three preschool children at home. If I talked on the phone for very long, they would begin to demand my attention. I collected a number of interesting items and kept them near the phone: blocks, crayons, scissors, coloring books, small plastic animals—all items that would occupy their attention near me, yet allow me to finish a conversation. I gave them these toys only when I talked on the phone, so the children came to view them as a privilege.

Your work is important. Supporting and encouraging productive human beings is a satisfying occupation. Few working people have the opportunity to see others reach their full potential as human beings through their efforts. That is the fulfillment of a homemaker.

Whether single, divorced, married, or widowed, consider your job an opportunity from God—to serve Him, to serve others, and to mature spiritually.

Chapter Fourteen

SPECIAL WORK CIRCUMSTANCES

Steve's schedule was irritating the entire family. His wife was edgy and tense; the children were tired of being quiet during the day, and they resented his absence from their activities. For three years Steve had worked the swing shift (four to midnight). To complicate the situation, it wasn't a Monday-to-Friday job, but rather Wednesday-to-Sunday. Steve left the house at 3:15 and returned about 12:45 in the morning. He tried to sleep till about 9:00, but usually the children awakened him. Until recently his wife, Kay, also worked. She left at 8:00, so there were several days when she and Steve hardly saw each other. Getting the children ready for school was a hassle; Steve didn't want to get up, and Kay was in a frantic rush.

Steve and Kay were Christians and wanted to be effective for God. But because of their schedules, they soon started losing touch in their relationships with people, with the church, and with each other. Their marriage relationship became strained. The children began to complain that they didn't feel as if they were really a family. The dilemma was that Steve felt lucky to have his job, and Kay's salary allowed the family to buy a few of the "extra" things.

About three months ago the situation erupted in a heated argument about money. Previous arguments had been about Steve's schedule, his sleep, or who would get the children ready for school. Steve always won—and felt terrible. This time Steve and Kay realized that both were losing. They admitted that they were both slipping spiritually and that the children were suffering. They made some significant changes that have revolutionized their family life. Kay quit her job. Steve reserved every Tuesday night for the family; he started getting up for breakfast with the family on Wednesday and Thursday. Steve and Kay planned to spend specific time together during the week and to give the weekend time for the children. Steve planned Bible study and other projects during the day. The changes revolutionized their lives. In fact, the whole family grew to like Steve's work schedule.

Steve and Kay encountered a special situation. In this chapter on unusual job circumstances, it is difficult to generalize and give categorical guidelines as in previous chapters. We mention only a few general advantages, disadvantages, and dangers. Then we include some specific suggestions in four categories:

▶ Shift worker
▶ Traveler
▶ Seasonal worker
▶ Self-employed

Advantages and Benefits
Unusual time available. Weekday evenings are the most difficult times to use effectively. Therefore, whenever job schedules allow extra days off during daytime hours, you have an opportunity to make good use of the time, since very little else would ever be scheduled in your community, your

church, or your family. With good planning, these unusual times can be used to great advantage.

Extra time off. Unless your job is regular shift work, a special schedule frequently allows for extra time off. However, seasonal work is not particularly an advantage unless you can engage in another job. An airline pilot, for example, could develop a business sideline or a significant ministry in his flexible time off. Whatever your circumstance, if you get extra time, learn how to use it constructively.

Better pay. Many firms pay higher wages to the person working on odd shifts or days. The wages may be worth the inconvenience.

Disadvantages and Restraints
Odd schedule. It becomes difficult to adjust permanently to an odd schedule, because it will always be out of phase with the rest of the community. Therefore a regular routine of living may be difficult to establish.

Family disruption. The rest of the family, being on a more normal schedule, may find that adjusting to yours is disrupting. Planning times for church and school activities invites frustration. The family may lack unity and cohesiveness. This impact is greatest on the mother who generally tries to hold things together in the home.

Spiritual Dangers
Making excuses. With unusual working schedules, it becomes easy to excuse yourself from church, family, or spiritual activities. Don't allow your peculiar circumstances to keep you from what may be most needful in your life.

Withdrawing. Since your schedule is either undependable or different, it is easy to withdraw gradually from spiritual fellowship and from vital contact in your community. You must make special efforts to keep involved.

Having mentioned the few items common to the unusual jobs, let us offer some specific suggestions for each category.

THE SHIFT WORKER

Any shift other than the common eight-to-five places unusual pressures on you and your family. Your sleep schedule becomes confused, family activities are difficult to coordinate, and regular weekly involvement in any activity is almost impossible. Yet, taking practical steps to counter the problems and taking advantage of the schedule may change your whole attitude and perspective. I have worked various shifts—the worst kind: my schedule was a ten-day cycle of two swing shifts, two midnight shifts, two day shifts, and then three and one-half days off. Some of these ideas helped me to adjust to that schedule:

Design your sleep schedule. Without adequate sleep, you cannot function properly. Your body has a built-in clock that is conditioned by habit, so you must help it adjust to your schedule. For swing shifts the change is not drastic: many workers function well on six or seven hours sleep with an occasional early afternoon nap and perhaps some extra weekend sleep. For the midnight-to-eight shift, the adjustment is more difficult, especially with a return to "normal" hours on the days off. Daytime sleep is probably best, though some function well on three hours before going to work and four or five in the morning after work. There is no easy adjustment for days off except to try to function on mixed sleep schedules with an occasional long (nine-or-ten-hour) period of sleep.

Do not expect the entire family to tiptoe around and be tense while you sleep. Remove the phone from the bedroom. Use ear plugs for noise reduction: get specific ones made, if necessary. A fan or a similar constant noise in the room masks other sounds. Some like to have a well-insulated room in the basement. It is helpful to have a doorbell that can be disconnected.

Use daytime hours well. For doing projects, studying, or running errands, the daytime hours are better than evenings. You face fewer interruptions and can generally use a four- or five-hour block. It is difficult to get even three consecutive hours in the evening. Your schedule will give the equivalent of two Saturdays. Apply the ideas mentioned earlier to your daily time off.

Adjust to weekends. It is critical to invest your days off in the family, since your presence during the week is greatly reduced. Try to flow with the family schedule rather than your own on weekends.

Give your mate a break. Your schedule will have almost as heavy an impact on your spouse as on you. As you will be around more during the day, use this time for caring for the children or doing specific tasks in the home. Don't make it seem that the whole world must adjust to your odd schedule.

Do not use your schedule as an excuse. Use your schedule as an advantage in getting more done, not as an excuse for not doing certain things. When I taught at the Air Force Academy, I knew how full a cadet's schedule was. At the beginning I was awed by it, thinking that they really had very little time to be involved in spiritual activities. But I soon discovered that if a cadet *really* wanted to do something, somehow he found the time and opportunity. If he wanted to ski, he would end up on the slopes most weekends with various clubs and activities. If you really *want* to do something, you can and will find time and opportunity. You can find time for your family, your own spiritual growth, and an outreach to others—*if* you want to. If you don't want to, no amount of free time will make it convenient.

THE TRAVELER

Regardless of the occupation, the person who travels a great deal faces special pressures and restrictions. I fit this category, for I am away from home about forty percent of the year. There are many things you can do to counter the problems raised in this kind of schedule. First let me note that many people travel even though they never leave town, that is, they are in so many evening and weekend activities that they might as well be gone. I too have made that mistake and had to come to grips with a hyperactive schedule.

Plan your travel. The further ahead you plan your travel, the better you and your family can adjust. But planning involves more than just scheduling in advance. Specifically we suggest that you

▶ space your trips so that you are home more frequently;

▶ try to avoid traveling on weekends;

▶ don't plan many long trips in any given year; even it if costs more, make shorter trips;

▶ set a limit on the time you are gone;

▶ keep records of your "away" time (I count a day away by the number of evenings I am gone, because evenings are most important to my family);

▶ try to avoid last-minute changes;

▶ plan travel around key activities of your family and your local spiritual ministries;

▶ plan less travel during the summer months.

I wish to emphasize your being home on key occasions and important activities of the family. Basketball games, choir concerts, and birthdays are more important to your children than you might think. Your schedule will tell your children how important they are to you.

Guard your mate's role. When you are gone, a heavy burden falls on your spouse. Financial decisions, child discipline, home maintenance, and myriad other things become the responsibility of the spouse who remains with the family. The pressure can be devastating. If you do not plan carefully, you both can step out of your biblical roles. During the Vietnam conflict, servicemen regularly had one-year tours of duty overseas. Many marriages were destroyed as wives were forced to assume total responsibility for their families and grew to enjoy their independence.

If you are a husband who travels, here are some ideas for helping your wife:

▶ Let her know where to reach you on any given day.

▶ Plan with her how the children are to be disciplined. Inform the children that you will be in touch continually and will be involved in discipline decisions. This is more important as the children become teenagers, since open rebellion and resistance tend to develop in the father's absence during those years.

▶ Enlist a friend or two to check on your family's needs in your absence.

▶ Make sure all your legal documents are in order in case of an emergency.

▶ Allow your wife financial freedom in your absence.

▶ Do not set standards for the children that your wife cannot enforce.

▶ Have a clear understanding of the kinds of situations in which she must call you.

▶ Give your family extra time when you return, perhaps including a special activity or function.

▶ Plan to give your wife free time from family responsibilities after a trip, even if it is only part of a day.

Morality. Every person experiences moral temptations, but the traveler is especially susceptible. Time alone, motel rooms, and available pornography all contribute to this problem. There also is the insidious thought that because you are off where you are unknown, no one will know what you have done. One serviceman told me, "When you are ten thousand miles from home, you soon think you are ten thousand miles from God." Jealously guard your eyes, mind, and body in this matter. Live on the basis of the promises of 1 Corinthians 10:13. One helpful thing is to witness daily to someone—let others know that your reputation is aligned with God's standards.

Use time well on the road. When you travel, you are away from customary commitments and often have extra free time. Plan constructive things to do: Bible study, Scripture memorization, correspondence. Accomplish things while traveling that will free your time once you return home. This will take planning for each trip. Also seek out Christian fellowship in the various places that you visit.

Take the children with you. Try to take each child with you once a year on a trip. You will have personal time with that child, and it will be an adventure for him or her. It will also help your children to understand some of the requirements of your work.

Use the phone. Call home frequently when you travel— daily, if possible. Talk to your children, not only your spouse. Your voice is the next best thing to your presence. You can handle many family decisions in this way. It *is* worth the cost. Your company may even allow this as a compensation for travel.

Special times with the family. When you travel a lot, special times with the family become even more important. Celebrating a birthday two days late *is* a problem to a seven-year-old. What the child thinks is important really is more crucial than what *you* think is important in his or her activities. Give special attention to vacations—make them family-centered.

Plan your time at home. When you are not traveling, try to spend extra time at home. Work shorter days if possible. Avoid traveling during school holidays or vacations. Remember that when you were gone, your spouse carried an extra load; thus you should plan on taking more responsibility in all areas when you are home.

THE SEASONAL WORKER

Many jobs are seasonal in nature and require maximum effort for only part of the year. Typical examples are construction workers, farmers, school teachers, and harvesters. A common characteristic of these jobs is that a person may not work at all during part of the year and the amount worked is not totally sufficient to meet the financial needs of the family. Here are some practical suggestions to cope with this circumstance.

Prepare for the seasonal push. Realize that during the working season, you will be pushed for time and will have to work harder and longer. Prepare both yourself and the family for that adjustment by spending additional time with them during the off-season.

Discipline yourself financially. Seasonal variation means financial fluctuation. It is imperative that you save some money to carry you over the off-season time. Many seasonal jobs have a degree of insecurity of future employment. Therefore, you need to avoid debt of any kind other than a home and medical needs.

Plan your off-season time. Depending on your financial needs, you must make definite plans for the off-season. Consider these ideas:

▶If finances permit, go to school or a training session to help you change your occupation to something more stable, or to make you more qualified in your present work.

▶Develop off-season sources of income. This would be an opportunity to begin some kind of business or other self-employment.

▶Give special consideration to your family, since they were likely neglected during your seasonal work push.

Stabilize your family. Family stability is extremely important. If it is necessary for you to change locations during your seasonal work or year by year, we suggest leaving the family in one place while you travel to the work location. Their stability is more important than your inconvenience for a short period.

Spiritual involvement and training. With extra time available, you have a good opportunity to devote time to your church or some community organization. It may give you the chance for some extensive spiritual training. Many churches, especially in larger cities, have special Bible training classes for laymen.

THE SELF-EMPLOYED

The American dream of a few decades ago was to have a small family business: to be independent, to be your own boss, to work and be paid directly for your product. With increased industrialization and the growth of large corporations, it has become more and more difficult to operate a small business profitably.

Yet the opportunity remains. Repair shops, small contractors, independent insurance agencies, laundromats, and many other kinds of businesses are prime examples. People are self-employed as doctors, lawyers, dentists, farmers, and other specialists.

Ron was an expert mechanic. Most of his life had been spent working for others, so he tried self-employment by leasing a service station. But he operated it on the thin edge of financial disaster: Ron had to pay his wholesaler cash, but his business was strained by his customers' outstanding accounts. People needed gas and repairs, and he couldn't say no, but still he had to pay his bills. Finally he sold out and went back to work for someone else as a mechanic.

During this time, Ron and his wife, Karen, began to experience trouble in their lives and marriage. They had undergone problems before, and this was a new flare-up of lifelong struggles. Their children were grown and married, so they seriously considered resolving the problems by divorce. In the midst of this crisis they were confronted with Christ as the answer to their needs. Karen's response was, "My father was an atheist. If he is going to hell, so am I!" Ron's response was indifference and pride: he didn't need outside help. Besides, most people he knew in churches were hypocrites, and he wanted no part of that.

But it became obvious that their needs were beyond help in the human sense. Karen finally received Christ, but struggled in spiritual growth. Ron delayed for three years but then became a Christian, too. After both made commitments, their life together really began to change. They became deeply involved in a church and shared a clear witness of the change Christ brought to their lives.

Almost concurrently with their commitment to Christ came the opportunity to buy the small repair business where Ron was employed. Because of their earlier failure they were hesitant, but after prayer and careful consideration they finally decided to go ahead. The results were phenomenal. They dedicated the business to God and determined to give generously from the profits. The business grew and prospered. There were new pressures and problems, but they had financial freedom they had never before experienced. The more they earned, the more they gave—even when the financial picture for that month looked bleak. God repeatedly blessed their steps of faith.

What made the difference between their first and second attempts at self-employment? I believe it was their decision to follow God's pattern for their personal lives and their business. God does have much to say about how to conduct business. Several factors are decisive in self-employment.

Advantages and Benefits

Freedom in responsibility. You are your own boss. You have obvious responsibilities, yet you can choose when and how much to work. You have the freedom to choose your employees, to witness on the job, and to limit or expand your work schedule.

Motivation. Most of us are highly motivated when we are "doing our own thing." When the success of the business depends directly on our labor, we are more motivated to perform well and to produce. Whether it is right or wrong, people are always more motivated to promote their own interests than the interests of another.

Finances. If the business is prospering, a self-employed person has greater financial freedom. All profits from the business are his. If he is skilled in the service he is performing, he will always earn more than if he is employed by another. For professional specialists like doctors and lawyers, the prospects of high income are very good.

Security. In the beginning phases of a business or profession, security is limited. However, as a business becomes established, it provides more security than most employment. This is especially important to a person nearing middle age who will often find it difficult to obtain employment on the open market.

Family. The entire family can actively participate in many small businesses. Working together can unify a family, if they do not become slaves to the business. Making the business succeed becomes an integral part of family life.

While having my car serviced recently, I remarked to the owner of the station on the striking resemblance between him and the boy pumping gas. "That's my son," he answered proudly. "He wanted a motorbike, and he worked here to earn it. 'Course it will be another year before he has his driver's license. For now, we work together. He helps me, and I think he's learning something."

Disadvantages and Restraints

Lack of freedom. This is the other side of the coin. Responsibility brings restriction. You are always on call. You may not be able to leave town any time you like. The customer effectively controls you—especially if business is slow. Even a doctor can't leave town unless his patients are covered by another physician.

Financial pressure. Many small businesses operate on a thin financial margin, especially in the early years. Taxes, rising costs of materials and labor, and the fluctuating economy all bring significant pressure. Profits may be great at times, but losses can prove devastating. A friend of mine told me how he was approached by the key employees in his business when it was finally paying off after several years of struggle. They wanted to put pressure on him for a profit-sharing agreement. My friend sent them back to their lawyer with the reply, "When you can include a loss-sharing clause, come and see me!" Many people simply do not want the uncertainty and hassle of financial insecurity and would rather not take the risk of self-employment.

Time pressure. In one sense, your time is never your own. You are always obligated to the customer. Your employees do not feel this stress, but you do. You must always be on call. You will face constant pressure to work longer hours and extra days. A mechanic is obligated to respond to his customer's needs; a farmer must harvest at the right time and in the right weather; a storekeeper must keep his shop open at the hours people find it convenient to shop. Time is always in short supply.

Total responsibility. If things go wrong, there is no one else to shoulder the blame. Finances, production, quality, mistakes, and dissatisfied customers all become your problems. That is why a self-employed person deserves the extra profit—for all the responsibility he bears. This is a heavy load, especially when problems develop.

Spiritual Dangers

Overwork. In your own business, extra work can easily replace many important things in your life. Those extra hours can hurt you emotionally, physically, and spiritually. The temptation is strong to "sell your soul to the company store" when it is your own company. Hard work is good; consuming work is wrong. Guard against allowing your own business to deprive you of your family, a spiritual outreach, and your very life.

Pride. As you become successful and more confident in your business, pride may invade your life as you view what you have accomplished. At this point remember that all you own and all you have accomplished come from God. What you possess is a trust from God to be used under His direction. You cannot assume credit for the ability He gave you to accomplish your work.

Finances. If you are successful in your self-employed

status, you are probably doing well financially. Don't allow money to control and drive you. A rich man was once asked how much money was enough. He replied, "Just a little more." Don't fall into the trap of allowing finances to become an end instead of a means. Chapter 7 provides further guidance on the use of money.

Anxiety. Ulcers seem to be the common denominator of independent businessmen. The total responsibility for success is on your shoulders, humanly speaking, and therefore worry and anxiety can become a way of life. If your self-employment leads to excessive worry, it may be an indication that you should not remain in that work circumstance. Fear, worry, and anxiety are paralyzing, both physically and spiritually. First Peter 5:7 says, "Casting all your anxiety upon Him, because He cares for you." Significantly, it is interesting to note that this verse is preceded by a command for humility and followed by a passage on resisting the Devil, standing firm in the faith and enduring suffering. Your witness shrinks as your anxiety increases, so you must learn to focus your dependence on God, not yourself. He is your only real means of peace and security.

Ethics. As mentioned earlier, ethics become a key issue when you can set the standards, guidelines, and prices in your work. The Bible stresses the need for ethical business practices, as summarized in Deuteronomy 25:14-15: "You shall not have in your house differing measures, a large and a small. You shall have a full and just weight; you shall have a full and just measure, that your days may be prolonged in the land which the LORD your God gives you." Be careful to give the full value of what you are being paid for. This means that your pricing principle cannot always be "what the market will stand." Jealously guard your honesty and ethics. It is better to lose a little money than to carry a nagging conscience.

Guidelines and Suggestions
Give your business to God. The first step in success as a self-employed person is to give your business to God. How do you do that? In prayer

> ▶ thank God for the business;
> ▶ acknowledge to God that the business is His;
> ▶ determine to operate on biblical principles and ethics;
> ▶ resolve to give to God's work as you are prospered;
> ▶ ask God to allow you and your business to be a clear witness for Christ;
> ▶ agree to put your family and your walk with Him before the business.

Remember that God does not promise unlimited business success, but He does promise to meet our needs (Matthew 6:33) and bless our lives (Ephesians 3:20, Philippians 1:6).

Limit your working hours. You must work hard, but you cannot give your whole life to your work. No business is worth destroying yourself physically, eliminating a spiritual outreach, or neglecting your family.

Guard your family. It is vitally important to guard your family from excessive involvement in the business. Your spouse or children must not be forced to give themselves to it inordinately. Don't allow the work to become a wedge in family relationships. Your family deserves far more attention than your business.

Give financially. As God prospers your business, give financially to His work. God's earthly resources are people and material goods. God does operate on a principle of sowing and reaping in every segment of life. If you sow sin, you will reap sin's reward. In 2 Corinthians 9:6, Paul speaks of finances when he says, "He who sows sparingly shall also reap sparingly; and he who sows bountifully shall also reap bountifully."

Use your position. Your position as a self-employed person in the community will bring you admiration and respect. Use that position as an influence for Christ. You have none of the restrictions sometimes imposed by large companies, so you can speak openly and freely on and off the job. Be involved in civic affairs. Influence your community.

Leave your work at work. Owning the business is no reason for it to plague your mind twenty-four hours a day. You must get away from it mentally as well as physically. Develop a hobby and a ministry to others. The pressures are great, but learn to discipline your mind and your time to find relief and relaxation from the job.

A standard of excellence. Know your business thoroughly. Make your work reflect the biblical standard of excellence (Colossians 3:23). In applying this standard you need to run your business on sound economic principles. A Christian is not to be an "easy mark" for cheaper performance; but give discounts when it will help your business or when you really want to contribute financially to a group or an individual.

Maintain an attitude of gratefulness for the privilege of owning and operating your own business. Allow God to demonstrate His place in your life by the way you operate day by day in your job.

Chapter Fifteen

AN EXCITING FUTURE

One person looks back at his past, looks at himself, then grumbles. He becomes fearful and withdraws, never wanting to face the reality of life again. Because of this he has begun to die.

Another person looks back, looks at himself, then looks to God and the future, and launches out with the mental fervor of youth and lives life to the fullest. He has been rejuvenated.

The difference between them is found in their view of the essence of life. For one man life means his future, not his past. His life is planted in a belief in the sovereign control of God. With this view, the future is as bright as the promises of God. Life is based on hope, not regret.

A positive mental and spiritual attitude brings every event into perspective through the light supplied by God's Word. In this concluding chapter we want to set the stage for your personal action in the years ahead.

As we conclude this study on work, take this time to think through the whole of your life—to bring it all into perspective.

PERSPECTIVE ON LIFE

We each develop a perspective on life as we grow older and gain experience. We develop attitudes and ideas that color our entire view of life. Several factors can help us develop a positive, dynamic attitude toward our personal future.

Time

> Time is the most undefinable yet paradoxical of things; the past is gone, the future has not come, and the present becomes the past even while we attempt to define it, and, like the flash of the lightning, at once exists and expires.[1]

Time is our most precious commodity. But none of us knows how much of it we possess. If we lament over the time that is gone, we will never learn to live in the present and prepare for the future. We learn from the past. We do not live in the past.

Time and age are inextricably related. Often, when we think of time we relate it to our age. We tend to think of how little rather than how much time we have. A life perspective that focuses on the present and the future provides a better view of life. We recount the blessings of God in the past, but we experience the blessings of God today. The past supplies wisdom and strength for today and tomorrow, but offers no means of changing our history.

God clearly teaches His perspective on time: "For a thousand years in Thy sight are like yesterday when it passes by, or as a watch in the night" (Psalm 90:4). Time is not the crucial issue for God. What counts with Him is character. He is interested in the person as well as what he does. God wants us to be aware that time is transient. The psalmist prayed,

"Show me, O LORD, my life's end and the number of my days; let me know how fleeting is my life. You have made my days a mere handbreadth; the span of my years is as nothing before you. Each man's life is but a breath" (Psalm 39:4-5, NIV). In view of life's brevity we pray, "So teach us to number our days, that we may present to Thee a heart of wisdom" (Psalm 90:12).

An awareness of time causes us to concentrate on serving God with the best of our lives. God wants us to live the years we have left to the maximum. He desires a full commitment to serving Him with both time and energy. Thus, when we view our time as God's time, we become stewards who spend it only as He directs. But more often we tend to focus on ourselves, our own comfort, desires, and plans, so that we drown God's will in a flood of self-satisfaction. Such a perspective leads only to regret and despair. Realizing the futility of doing anything else rather than serving God gives a new hope and purpose to the future.

Wherever we are in life, particularly if we are a bit older, we have a unique set of experiences upon which we can build for the future. We can minister to others on the basis of what God has done in our lives. Thankfulness and anticipation should make our perspective. Let's live today to the fullest by serving God, and putting the past and the future into God's perspective on life.

Blaise Pascal, the French mathematician, wrote,

Let any man examine his thoughts, and he will find them ever occupied with the past or the future. We scarcely think at all of the present; or if we do, it is only to borrow the light which it gives for regulating the future. The present is never our object; the past and the present we use as means; the future only is our end. Thus, we never live, we only hope to live.[2]

Being a Learner

Cato, the Roman scholar, started studying Greek when he was over eighty. Someone asked why he tackled such a difficult task then. "It's the earliest age I have left," said Cato, and went right on studying. When a person stops learning, he begins dying. Sadly, only rarely does he realize that he is dying. The secret of finding happiness and fulfillment in life, apart from direct spiritual renewal, is being a learner. The one who constantly seeks to learn and develop will never dry up emotionally or mentally.

The author of Proverbs wrote, "A wise man will hear and increase in learning, and a man of understanding will acquire wise counsel" (Proverbs 1:5). On the other hand, "Fools despise wisdom and instruction" (Proverbs 1:7).

A hallmark of youth is the desire and ability to learn. But something strange happens as we grow older. We should know many things, but we feel we do not. We should be wise, but we may not be. Pride keeps us from revealing our need, and we close our minds to new ideas and teaching. When we lose our ability or our desire to learn, we seal our fate and shrivel and fade. But if we continue to develop and expand our knowledge, experience, and abilities, we will keep growing. For the person who remains a learner, there is no limit to the potential of life at any age.

Thus, being a learner gives a positive, rejuvenating perspective on life that will sustain us through any adversity.

Learning to Live with Stress

Stress is a reality of life. It always has been. All that changes over the years is the growing respect and appreciation for the effects of stress. In a Harvard study on aging, the one common contributor to good physical and emotional health was reported to be the ability to respond well to stress. The adverse consequences of stress are ulcers, heart trouble, high blood pressure, depression, and many other physical and emotional illnesses.

A healthy perspective on life views stress as normal, but temporary. In fact, it is not the stress itself that causes the problems, but our emotional response to it. Each personality type tends to respond differently to various stresses. Some fight. Others worry and fret. Others become angry. Some withdraw or quit. A few press on as though the stresses did not exist.

Regardless of how mature and spiritual we may be, we will all respond initially to stress according to our personality and background. The key is what follows the initial response. If we continue to react negatively, we will suffer. But if we are alert to stress and respond biblically, we can avoid its negative effects.

"Be anxious for nothing, but in everything by prayer and supplication with thanksgiving let your requests be made known to God. And the peace of God, which surpasses all comprehension, shall guard your hearts and your minds in Christ Jesus" (Philippians 4:6-7). This is one of the most practical promises in Scripture for our emotional peace of mind. Applying it is not as easy as quoting it, however. The promise is rooted in the sovereignty of God. If you learn to live with stress, you will greatly enhance your enjoyment and fulfillment in life.

YOUR PLAN FOR THE FUTURE

The great manufacturer Charles Kettering said, "My interest is in the future because I am going to spend the rest of my life there."[3] The future comes whether we want it to or not. Will we welcome it with a ready plan and purpose, or fight it, resenting its intrusion with fear and trepidation? God promises us power to live: "His divine power has granted to us *everything* pertaining to life and godliness, through the true knowledge of Him who called us by His own glory and excellence" (2 Peter 1:3).

All of our personal life experiences have prepared us for a future under God's direction. Without God's direction and control, we will have very little hope or encouragement. Without His control our lives are rootless and shifting. If we live under His control, we have an eternal point of reference and direction.

Now is the time for self-evaluation. To make a plan for your future, you need to know where you are *now*. Self-evaluation is not easy, for we are frequently blind to our own needs. Evaluate yourself with the help of your spouse or a close friend. Briefly review the previous chapters and make some extra notes on your key personal needs. Evaluate not only your work and career, but your entire life.

Consider the charts in Figures 15-1 and 15-2, which are on pages 293 and 294. Make a copy of these to fill out, or use the ones in this book. The purpose of the chart in Figure 15-1 is to help you identify issues you are experiencing now. Figure 15-2 will help you determine an overall picture of both your past and present. After completing these evaluations, choose several areas in which you would like to develop. Then select one or two of these areas to begin developing first. You may want to refer to suggestions in the earlier chapters for specifics in various areas that you are concerned about.

The keys to effectively making any kind of change are:

▶Recognize and admit your need.
▶Carefully define your need.
▶Make a decision to take positive steps to meet the need.
▶Begin a plan of action, *now*.

Use the format in Figure 15-3 (page 295) for your personal development plan. For example:

> *Description of need:* We have been communicating less and less as husband and wife. We have noticed increasing irritability and conflict. We are so busy at church, on the job, and with our children that we don't have enough time together.
>
> *Ideas on how to meet the need:* Talk daily. Have dinner alone once a week. Get a weekend away. Set aside one night a week to be together. Drop one activity. No overtime for one month. Read a book together on communication.

SPECIFIC PLANS	START BY	COMPLETE BY
1. Go to dinner to discuss a plan to improve communication.	Next weekend	Same
2. Set aside at least five minutes per day for talking privately.	Next Monday	Continue
3. Read *Getting to Know You*.	Nov. 5	Dec. 5
4. Plan two days away together.	Set date by Nov. 15	Jan. 15

Another example:

> *Description of need:* I have been very tired and down emotionally. I know I am overweight and eating poorly. I think at least part of my problem is poor nutrition and a lack of exercise.
>
> *Ideas on how to meet the need:* Have a physical examination. Start an exercise program. Improve my eating habits. Start jogging. Develop better sleep habits.

SPECIFIC PLANS	START BY	COMPLETE BY
1. Begin walking one mile each day for five of seven days a week.	Tomorrow	Continue
2. Get a physical check-up.	Mar. 1	Same
3. Begin my jogging program.	Day after physical exam	Continue four times per week
4. Stop snacking.	Now	Continue
5. Reduce the amount of food I eat (by one moderate helping), and by cutting sweets and starches out of my diet.	Begin now and taper off again in two weeks.	Check progress each month.

We want to emphasize that if you do not make a plan (it doesn't *have* to be written), you very likely will not do anything about your need. Wishful thinking should never substitute for action.

Along with the areas you identified for yourself, we suggest that you set some goals in the following areas.

Examine your *personal relationship with God* to see if you are becoming a spiritually mature person. The joy and freedom of maturity gives a confidence and satisfaction that nothing else can give. Pick some particular area of your spiritual life to develop and improve.

Next, look at your *marriage relationship*. Patterns and problems that are not changed or corrected now will probably not change later.

Finally, remember that your life is not complete without some *ministry to others*. God does not want any of us to live only for ourselves. Even when we are doing well spiritually, have an excellent marriage, and good family relationships, the absence of a personal ministry to others severely dulls the enjoyment that could exist.

IDENTIFYING CURRENT ISSUES

1. List some of the issues that you are currently struggling with.

_____

_____

_____

_____

_____

2. Choose one or two of these issues that are of the greatest concern to you now.

_____

_____

3. What problem areas do you feel you have resolved to your satisfaction?

_____

_____

4. What one area is crucial to begin work on immediately?

_____

_____

Figure 15-1

EVALUATION

Issues	Stable	Has Been or Is a Problem	Changing	Needs Changes
Priorities				
Contentment				
Witness				
Ministry				
Attitude toward success				
Spiritual foundations				
Finding God's will				
Work circumstances				
Other				

Figure 15-2

DEVELOPMENT PLAN

Description of need: _____

_____

_____

Ideas on how to meet the need:_____

_____

_____

Specific Plans	Start By	Complete By
1. _____ _____		_____
_____		
2. _____ _____		_____
_____		
3. _____ _____		_____
_____		
4. _____ _____		_____
_____		

Figure 15-3

One of the most encouraging and emotionally uplifting activities of life is personal development and education. When life stagnates, new inputs will stimulate and encourage us. Whether the development relates to job or personal life matters little. What counts is an aggressive, constructive development. Correspondence courses, night classes, craft schools, and reading can all be part of your learning plan. Part of being a learner is to keep exploring. Seek out positive new experiences. Do things you have never tried before. Learn new subjects, skills, and activities individually, as a couple, and as a family.

We took a short Greek course together. Jerry took skiing lessons with our son, Steve. Mary began learning violin with one of our daughters. Other couples learn tennis together or read books and discuss them. Some build a new addition onto their house. Never stop learning, developing, and growing.

As part of your plan for the future, develop relationships with younger people. Most of us minister downward in age. We can have significant relationships with younger people. Of course, you aren't going through the same things they are, but you did once, and it was not long ago. Many young couples would welcome a sincere friendship with an older couple. You may wonder how you can do this since you move in different social circles. Here are some ideas:

▶ Initiate the relationships by inviting young couples to your home or to some event.
▶ Use your children as a point of contact. Your youngest may be the age of a younger couple's oldest child.
▶ When asked for advice and counsel, do all you can to give helpful, practical advice and suggestions.
▶ Find mutual interests and activities.
▶ Don't expect an exclusive relationship with younger

couples, since they will also have peer relationships.

▶ Don't try to dress and act young or chic. Dress and act your age and let your maturity attract them.

▶ Study the Bible with younger couples or in separate men's or women's groups.

▶ Extend your friendship, help, and concern unselfishly and relationships will develop naturally.

We greatly value our friendship and interests with those our own age. But we would be far poorer if we did not have a number of close friendships with younger singles and couples. They need our maturity and experience. We need their youthful challenge and stimulation.

SOME FINAL THOUGHTS

You know by now that we consider work, life, worship, ministry, and family as one integrated whole. Even though we dissect them and try to improve each one, they cannot really be separated. In particular, your work and career hold equal importance with worship and ministry—because they *are* worship and ministry. They are the arena in which you minister and witness—particularly when held in balance with your family and personal walk with God.

The next time you go to work, go with the objective that God called you and equipped you for that very task.

NOTES: 1. Charles Caleb Colton, in *The International Encyclopedia of Thought* (Chicago: J.G. Ferguson Publishing Co., 1969), page 723.

2. Blaise Pascal, in *The International Encyclopedia of Thought*, page 581.

3. Charles Franklin Kettering, in *The International Encyclopedia of Thought*, page 315.

4. Dr. Raymond C. Ortlund, *The Best Half of Life* (Glendale, Calif.: Gospel Light/Regal Books, 1979).